THE YOUNG LEARNER'S HANDBOOK

THE YOUNG LEARNER'S HANDBOOK

STEPHEN TCHUDI

Charles Scribner's Sons · New York

Title page illustration by Mike Stromberg.
Illustrations on pages 7, 11, 23, 30 and 122 by Jackie Aher.

Charles Scribner's Sons Books for Young Readers
Macmillan Publishing Company
866 Third Avenue, New York, NY 10022
Collier Macmillan Canada, Inc.

Printed in the United States of America
First Edition
10 9 8 7 6 5 4 3 2

Library of Congress Cataloging-in-Publication Data
Tchudi, Stephen, 1942–   The young learner's handbook.
   Bibliography: p.
   Includes index.
   Summary: Explores the areas of expanding knowledge, gathering data, applying information, and developing a curious mind.

   1. Learning—Juvenile literature.
2. Thought and thinking—Juvenile literature.
3. Problem solving in children—Juvenile literature.
4. Research—Juvenile literature.   [1. Learning—Psychology.
2. Thought and thinking.   3. Problem solving.   4. Research]   I. Title.
LB1060.T35   1987   370.15'23   87-4523
ISBN 0-684-18676-4

for Ann Judy
a model young learner

Contents

Introduction   xi

1 Questing—The Idea of Independent Learning   1

Though there's much to be learned in school, there are
many times when you will want to master a subject on your
own. This chapter provides an introduction to **Questing**, a
process to help you expand your general knowledge, improve your skills, extend your hobbies, and enlarge your
knowledge through independent learning.

2 The Art of Questioning   17

Learning often begins with good questions. How to separate trivial from important questions. Techniques for creating questions: ballooning and brainstorming. Lateral
thinking. Separating little questions from big ones. Big
questions grown from little ones. Getting ready to search
for answers. Some world championship unanswered questions. Some questions for starting points.

3 Data Gathering   35

The importance of storing information systematically. Collecting objects or artifacts. Saving on paper: files, notes, journals, logs, drawings. The **Questpak.** Using media to gather data: audio recorders, film cameras, video cameras and recorders, computers.

4 Look It Up—Print and Media Sources   59

A guide to finding information in storage. Exploring the library. Learning from nonfiction, fiction, biography, books written for young adults. Some useful and curious reference books. Special collections, magazine files, clippings, films and video materials. Finding materials in bookstores. Learning from magazines and newspapers. Creating a library at home.

5 Learning from People   81

How to use people as an information source. The art of the interview. Whom to ask. Questioning techniques. Taking surveys and polls. How to learn from people's answers. Telephones as a research tool. Letter writing to obtain information. Computer bulletin boards.

6 Learning from Places   102

What you can learn from schools, colleges and universities, local government offices, county records, state and federal governments, museums and exhibits, local businesses, charitable and public service institutions, service organizations, hobbyist clubs.

7 Learning from Research   118

Conducting research when other information sources have been exhausted. The scientific method: questioning, collecting data, making hypotheses. Experimental research methods. Drawing conclusions. Applying research to problems. Unexplained problems. Research and the twenty-first century.

8 Applying What You Learn   135

Putting your learning skills to use in everyday situations. How to use knowledge as an aid to decision making. Problem solving techniques. Inventing. Achieving your aims and goals. Planning your leisure time. Predicting the future.

9 Sharing What You Know   158

Presenting ideas and information to people. Exhibits and displays. Speeches, talks, and demonstrations. Photographs and slide tapes. Films and videos. Writing as a way to share knowledge.

Appendix: Forming a QUESTARS Club   175

Bibliography   179

Index   183

Introduction

This *Young Learner's Handbook* is for "young" learners of any age who want to know more about the world in which they live. It describes ways of identifying and solving problems through the use of brainpower: study, imagination, creativity. This a "how to" book that gives you some ways to go about mastering new ideas and skills and putting all of your mind to work.

It's important to note that any person who picks up *The Young Learner's Handbook* already has mastered some powerful learning skills. For one thing, you obviously know how to read. Do you realize what a remarkable skill reading is? Scholars called psycholinguistists, who combine the study of thinking [psychology] and the study of language [linguistics], have learned that just to speak English (let alone *read* it) a person has to distinguish among some two hundred different sounds called *phonemes:* the sounds like "ah," "eh," "buh," "kuh," that can be strung together in endless combinations to create the words of our language. You learned to do that by the time you were two or three years old.

On top of that, the speaker of English has mastered something like four thousand different ways of combining words into phrases, phrases into sentences. When you first began speaking you were limited to short expressions like "ma ma" and "da da" and "goo goo," but by the time you were four you could string together full-size "grownup" sentences and you possibly began to read a few words that you saw in print regularly.

Then, about the time you started first grade you started to get serious about reading. You knew the alphabet, of course, but you also began to discover the ways in which those twenty-six letters could be combined in literally millions of words to create written sentences. You learned that something like this made sense: "Look behind you." But if you saw something like this: "Mcbr5z%y p&o fg6i 'o#b n 9lk3jkkl," you realized that it made no sense—not to you, and probably not to anybody else (at least anybody who spoke or read the English language). You could read.

Reading—what you are doing at this very moment—involves so many language skills that it is literally impossible to describe what goes on in people's minds as they read.

You learned this incredibly complicated skill mostly on your own. Of course you had coaching and advice from parents and teachers, but in the end, *you* learned all those complicated relationships by exploring your experience with language. Your abilities at speaking and reading (not to mention writing), open up the possibilities for learning, because most of what you know and discover will come to you, in one way or another, through language.

Thus as you begin *The Young Learner's Handbook,* you are an accomplished learner already, a master of your "mother tongue."

You are also a skilled learner in other ways. You presumably know how to tie your shoes. (If you think that's not much of an accomplishment, find a little person who doesn't know how and try to teach him or her.) You know how to guess at the weather by peering out the window and studying the clouds. You probably have hobby skills: perhaps you can recognize different kinds of birds or butterflies or fish on sight, or you can play a musical instrument or sing or dance, or you can work with tools and wood or with needles and thread. If you were suddenly faced with a new problem or a situation—say a baby elephant in your living room—you could figure out or learn what to do next, which shows you have developed some problem-solving skills.

Do you need a *Young Learner's Handbook* then? If you are already such a skilled learner, why examine this book?

It has often been said, "A little learning is a dangerous thing." Knowing only a small amount about something can create more problems than knowing a great deal about it. Thomas Huxley, a scientist who wrote in the middle of the last century, added, "If a little knowledge is dangerous, where is the man who has so much as to be out of danger?" ("On Elementary Instruction in Physiology," 1877, Lewis, p. 142).* People can never feel so confident about their knowledge that they can afford to stop learning. Robert Maynard Hutchens, a thinker in our own time, has suggested that we need a learning society made up of people who are committed to inquiry and discovery every day of their lives. *The Young Learner's Handbook* is intended to help you become an even better learner by putting together the skills you already have and by adding some new ones.

John Wooden, who coached basketball at the University of California Los Angeles (and won more college championships than anybody else) once said, "It's what you learn after you know it all that counts" (*They Call Me Coach,* Lewis, p. 149). What he meant (I believe) is that there is more to learning than just piling up knowledge and information. This handbook will help you learn how to make good use of your knowledge, thinking beyond just plain facts to figure out applications in your own life.

I don't claim that you'll be a smarter person after you've finished *The Young Learner's Handbook* or that you will be some sort of a walking encyclopedia. However, you will have a better understanding of what you know, and you'll probably have a good deal more con-

---

* All the authors referred to in this book are listed in the bibliography. If you want to find out more about any book or author listed in parentheses (such as Lewis, p. 142), just check the bibliography.

fidence about tackling new and unfamiliar learning tasks, both in school and outside.

In the first chapter I will introduce you to a process for learning called **Questing.** I will invite you to think of all your learning as a **Quest,** a voyage of discovery. In that chapter, and throughout the rest of the book, I will offer a number of suggestions for **Quest** topics and show you how to make a list of your own interests.

In Chapter 2 I will discuss how to get a **Quest** started through developing good **Quest**ions that use all the imaginative powers of your mind. Chapter 3 tells about data gathering and record keeping, which might not sound so interesting at first, conjuring up images of file cabinets stuffed full of paper or dreary notebooks filled with scribbles. However, as you'll see, keeping accurate track of your learning is important in and out of school, and there are ways of keeping records that can even be fun.

Chapters 4 through 7 discuss the major sources of information: books and other stored data, people, places (like museums and businesses), your own research.

In Chapters 8 and 9, I will help you think about some intriguing questions: "How can I apply what I know in my everyday life?" How can I share what I know with other people?"

It is important for people to become actively involved in learning, so I have built in some suggestions from time to time, say, to list ideas or questions, to find a book on a topic, or to pick up the phone and get some information. On the facing page is an example to get you started.

You'll also find another kind of **Questing** set off from the text of *The Young Learner's Handbook.* As personal computers have become popular and less expensive, more and more young learners have access to them, either at home or at school. A computer can be a wonderful aid to learning, letting you keep records, communicate with libraries and people, write reports, or sift through notes and other materials. For those readers who have access to a computer, I have included sections labeled **ComputerQuest.** If you don't use a computer, you might want to skip over these sections. However,

---

✳ ✳ ✳ QUESTING ✳ ✳ ✳

To organize for the learning that you will do as an outgrowth of this book, keep a notebook or learning log. I'll call it The Learner's Notebook. I suggest that you get a loose-leaf, three-ring binder or perhaps a portfolio or "trapper" with lots of pockets. As you proceed, you can put notes, clippings, or other material you collect into separate categories. To begin, make yourself a list of some of the areas where you *already* have strong interests. Jot down answers to the following:

What are your hobbies? What do you collect? Do you study nature? sports? people? pets?

What are your special skills and abilities? Do you play sports? Play an instrument? Write music or stories? Paint?

What school subjects do you like best?

How do you spend leisure time outside of school?

List your favorite TV shows. Write down the names of rock music or movie stars you particularly enjoy.

What do you know more about than anyone else in your family?

What do you know more about than most of your friends?

This is a short inventory of your special interests. Label that section of your Learner's Notebook "Ideas and Interests." Keep adding to it as you read and think.

---

don't feel left out if you are not a computerphile. Much of what you do with a computer can also be done with plain old paper and pencil. In some cases, keeping ideas on paper is even faster than a computer and safer, since handwritten materials don't disappear when somebody pulls an electric plug. All readers may want to read sections like the following just as a source of more possibilities for learning.

✳ ✳ ✳ COMPUTERQUEST ✳ ✳ ✳

Computer users can keep a Learner's Notebook using a personal computer. For example, you can use the word processing program to take notes and record ideas. To begin, you can create a word processing file of your interests as suggested in the **Questing** section earlier in the introduction. As you proceed through the book, you can establish separate files just as you might maintain separate sections in a three-ring notebook. With the computer it becomes easy to add materials and rearrange them, so the computer can function for you as a very flexible notebook. You can also print out the pages from time to time and maintain a regular paper notebook as a backup for your electronic files.

Above all, *The Young Learner's Handbook* is meant to be a guide to exploring ideas. You may want to read the book cover to cover and then set off learning on your own. I suspect, however, that you'll find this is a book you'll want to read in sections and return to from time to time. You can get ideas from various chapters and skip around from one chapter to another. In fact, you may want to begin by reading the Appendix, which comes last. It suggests some ideas for forming a **Questars** club, in which several learners get together to explore ideas they share in common. I think you'll find learning with a group of people who all like to expand their knowledge is even more exciting than going at it all on your own.

Whether you work in a club or by yourself, I hope you'll find this book useful in getting you involved in an activity that is as old as humankind—learning. *The Young Learner's Handbook* offers membership in a club that contains millions of members (but requires paying no dues), the community of learners worldwide.

THE YOUNG LEARNER'S HANDBOOK

1 Questing—The Idea of Independent Learning

The process I'll describe throughout this book for learning things on your own is called **Questing.** This is not a fixed or rigid procedure, and there are no set rules to follow. Anytime you want to learn something new you can call it a **Quest,** no matter how you go about it. Or, if you don't like the term "Quest," you can simply talk about "learning." By using the term **Quest,** however, and always highlighting it in bold face type in this book, I want to remind you of the spirit of independent learning, which begins with curiosity, with **Questing** after new ideas, experiences, and information.

Eleanor Roosevelt once remarked, "I think, at a child's birth, if a mother could ask a fairy godmother to endow it with the most useful gift, that gift would be curiosity" (*Today's Health,* October 2, 1966, Lewis, p. 70). Actually, most of us were born curious about our world and the people who live there, and it is natural to ask questions—to be curious—about the world in which we live. Have you nearly been driven crazy by a younger brother or sister who asked questions constantly? Or have you ever almost driven your parents or older brothers and sisters bonkers with questions of your own? Questions are a telltale sign of human curiosity at work.

1

Sometimes you hear people talk about "idle curiosity." As Leo Rosten once said, "The one thing that curiosity cannot be is idle" ("The David Susskind Show," February 19, 1978, Lewis, p. 70). Although asking questions can sometimes get on other people's nerves, asking good questions is a real art, and young (and older) learners ought to practice it all they can.

Buckminster Fuller was one of the great thinkers of our time. His ingenuity led him to invent, among other things, the geodesic dome, an architectural style that uses geometric principles in its design and requires much less structural support than conventional buildings. Fuller was delivering lectures when he was eighty years old, dazzling audiences by showing his own intellectual curiosity at work. He demonstrated clearly that elderly people can still be young learners. "Bucky" Fuller (whose book, *An Operating Manual for Spaceship Earth,* is one you might like to read), said that our principal purpose in life is to explore our planet and come to know it and ourselves better.

Much of your learning in coming years will be done in school, with teachers guiding you to explore ideas, facts, and concepts that are important for knowing about the world and for preparing for a job. However, there will be times—many times—when you want to learn beyond school. You may want to discover more about circles or painting or dinosaurs or radar or ghosts or motorcycles or lawsuits or exercise. You may find either that the ideas aren't covered in what you're studying or that you need to know more than the material supplied in your schoolbooks. At that point, you'll need to "know how to know."

There may be times when you're doing something with a club or hobby and need to know more. You may be working on a project for your scout troop or 4-H club and realize that you need information. You may be writing a play for your family and friends and run out of ideas, or you may be deeply engrossed in your hobby—say, butterfly collecting or quiltmaking—and recognize that you need to move beyond your present level of skill. Whenever that happens—or at any of the other thousands of times when questions pop into your mind—you're ready to embark on a **Quest.**

Webster's dictionary defines "quest" as a search, pursuit, or a seeking. It is related to the root word of *question* (the Latin *quaerere,* to seek or ask) which is at the heart of the **Questing** process.

"Questing" also was significant during the Middle Ages, "when knighthood was in flower." We know that an aspect of knighthood was a quest: to rescue or depose a king or to find the Holy Grail (a cup from which Jesus was said to have drunk) or to rescue a fair maiden. There are even reports—myths and legends, actually—of knights who set forth on quests to slay dragons. The days of knighthood have, unfortunately, been romanticized in stories and films. Those days were actually violent, grim, and dirty. Imagine how hot a man would become inside a heavy suit of armor, and imagine the fear and pain of battling another man with a broadsword or ax. We are in some ways more civilized now, and knighthood in England today has become largely ceremonial, a reward to people who have served their country. Nevertheless, we have inherited the spirit of seeking that is the heart of a **Quest.**

In his book, *The Aims of Education,* the British philosopher Alfred North Whitehead has written of the "romance" that accompanies learning. You've probably experienced the excitement and joy of getting involved in a new idea, of discovering amazing information in books or magazines, of getting so wound up in an idea that you are "lost in thought" or drift into daydreams. When that happens, you're engaged in the romance of a learning **Quest.**

Learning can be exciting and just plain *fun.* Of course there are also times when learning involves hard work. Alfred North Whitehead said that there must be *discipline* to accompany the romance of learning, and there are times when you will just have to "burn the midnight oil" over your books. Combining the natural pleasure of learning with occasional hard work often leads, however, to an even richer kind of understanding and depth of knowledge.

Getting Started: Creating Your Own Learning Center

Just as the medieval knight had certain "tools" that he carried on his quest—his armor, shield, and sword—a modern-day **Quester** has tools that make exploration and discovery easier: books, pencils and rulers, a globe, a microscope, binoculars, pliers and screwdrivers, needles and thread, magazines, photographs, cameras, cassette recorders, and perhaps a typewriter or computer. In school your teacher may have created a learning center, a convenient place to work on projects. Such a center may have a comfortable chair or carpet squares for relaxation while reading and thinking, a desk or table for writing, bookshelves filled with good and interesting reading, and possibly an aquarium or terrarium or ant colony. There may be an old typewriter or a new computer at the school learning center, along with plenty of paper, pencils, and art supplies. A learning center is a place where you can concentrate on what you're doing while having the tools of the learning trade close at hand.

To begin **Questing,** you might want to create a learning center at home—a place where it's easy for you to work on your hobbies, your school assignments, the questions you see as important. This center can be plain or fancy, depending on how often you work there and what you want to accomplish. At its simplest, a learning center might be just a study desk. On the other hand, it might be an elaborate build-it-yourself cubby with all sorts of specially designed shelves, nooks, and crannies for your stuff.

If you like building things, your center might include a workbench where you keep some tools for projects or a craft table for work on hobbies that range from building model ships to making jigsaw puzzles. It could include a bulletin board to display your artwork or to hang blueprints and plans; it might include a small museum or zoo where you keep objects or animals. If you're lucky enough to have a computer at home, you might ask if you can install it at your learning center. You'll certainly want to have storage space to keep all your notebooks and files, and you may want to have a shelf for some basic reference materials: a dictionary, a one-volume encyclopedia, a fact-book or almanac, your copy of *The Young Learner's Handbook.*

Most learning centers are built around some sort of table or other flat surface. You might be able to use a card table or folding table you have around the house, or you could possibly build a table out of some plywood and some store-bought legs. Many learners like to have a lot of open space with flat surfaces to spread out books and tools and papers when they're working on a project. Others want to have many bins or baskets or empty cardboard boxes where they can keep all the materials from their various projects in order, eliminating the clutter.

Whether you're a person who spreads things out or one who puts them away, you'll need plenty of storage. You don't have to be a neatness freak to want to be able to find your tools and resources, whether you're looking for the formaldehyde jar for butterflies or the special needles you use for embroidery. If you work mostly with books, shelving and bookcases will be an important feature of your learning center. If you are principally a collector, you might want to have a great many tin cans or plastic containers.

One good idea is to use collections of cardboard tubes (the sort you find on the inside of aluminum foil or plastic wrap rolls) tied together to form a bundle of hollows into which you can put rolled-up papers or various kinds of long and slender objects—from snake skins to arrows. Also check your local variety or department store for various kinds of plastic tubs, jars, drawers, cabinets, and boxes. You might want to buy some of these items for storage—plastic potato bins, "lazy Susan" spinners, shelf expanders, little boxes for screws and nails. However, once you've seen the commercial units, you can probably figure out how to make similar gizmos out of scrap or re-cycled material. You can also study how the storekeeper sets up and displays merchandise using clever (and often hand-built) shelves and boxes.

It's fun to scavenge for learning center materials. If your family or a neighbor is throwing out an old easy chair, you may be able to get it for your center and make a fresh cover for it. Garage or apartment sales are a terrific place to find used tables, shelving, and even lighting for your center. If you want a carpet, you may be able to find a used one cheap or to pick up some carpet remnants at a store. Cardboard is an excellent building material for learning centers, and you can use leftover cardboard boxes, large and small, for storage, for bulletin boards, or even for screens or walls to give you some privacy. Leftover paint can be applied to your center to give it a fresh look.

Some sample designs for learning centers are shown in Figure 1-1.

---

* * * QUESTING * * *

Design a learning center for yourself. Begin by figuring out where you'll put it. Use a ruler or yardstick to determine how much space you have available and then think about possible layouts. Make a list of what you most need when you work on projects of your own: books, materials, fix-it supplies, kits and models, etc. Look at the designs in Figure 1-1; then take off on your own to design your own unique place for learning and studying.

Become a scavenger, looking for castoff objects and materials. What use could you make of wood scraps, pillows, cardboard boxes, plastic boxes, empty tissue boxes, coffee cans, fabric scraps, old envelopes and greeting cards, bottle tops, can tops, or computer paper? However, don't get so absorbed in creating the learning center that you stop reading this book—plunge ahead!

Learning How You Learn

More important than the physical learning center are the *processes* or *procedures* that you follow in learning. The critical "learning center" that you have is the three-and-a-half-pound computer you carry around inside your skull—the brain.

FIGURE 1-1: Learning Centers

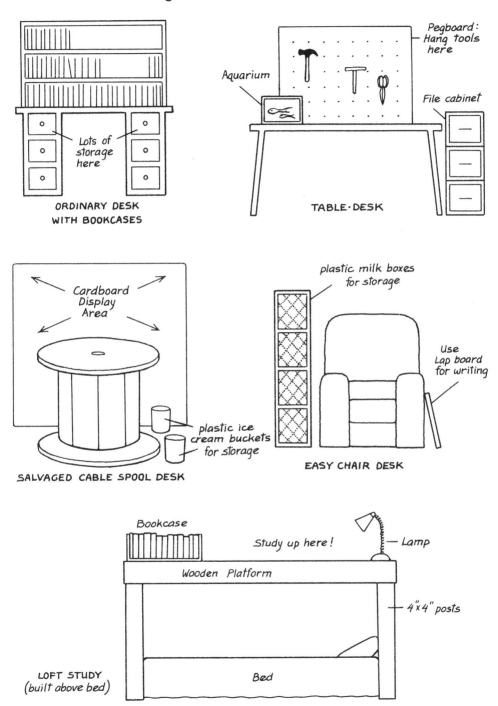

ORDINARY DESK WITH BOOKCASES

Lots of storage here

Pegboard: Hang tools here

Aquarium

File cabinet

TABLE·DESK

Cardboard Display Area

plastic ice cream buckets for storage

SALVAGED CABLE SPOOL DESK

plastic milk boxes for storage

Use Lap board for writing

EASY CHAIR DESK

Bookcase

Study up here!

Lamp

Wooden Platform

4"x4" posts

LOFT STUDY (built above bed)

Bed

People go about using their brains in many different ways. Some of us are "book learners"; that is, we like to see ideas in print. (One of my friends learned how to build an entire house, including the plumbing and wiring, just by studying books. He says that if you can *read,* you can learn to do just about anything.)

Some people are *visual* learners; they like to see diagrams and pictures. They can learn quickly and easily from television, films, and photographs—often more quickly than by studying a book. Some folks are *aural* learners, picking up information best by ear. (Remember that for centuries, especially before the invention of the printing press, humankind relied almost entirely on word of mouth to pass along information, ideas, and stories. An "oral culture" is still extremely common in many parts of the world, including the United States.) There are *tactile* learners, the "hands on" people who figure out things best by doing them. Some of us learn *intuitively,* operating largely on hunches and feelings about how things work. Others of us are *discovery* learners, figuring out things as we go along, and still others are *rule* or *principle* learners, who like to have somebody explain the general ideas first before they plunge into a job.

I hope that as you read this book you'll discover that you have more ways of learning than you knew. Human beings are terribly clever at figuring things out: researching medical cures, inventing technological devices, finding new ways of expressing ideas in music, art, film, and dance. As a member of the human race, you should use all the different modes of learning that are available to you through the learning center of your brain.

The Questing *Pattern*

The broad pattern of learning that I call a **Quest** works this way:
   · Asking questions
   · Looking for resources
   · Collecting and analyzing information
   · Sharing conclusions

---

* * * QUESTING * * *

Analyze how you learn. Start with school. In which classes do you seem to pick up ideas most easily? (Ignore for the moment the fact that some subjects interest you more than others; the point here is to think about your own method of learning.) Do you prefer reading something in a book to a class discussion? Would you rather study on your own or listen to the teacher talk? Would you prefer to read a *text*book or a *library* book or to see a *movie?* When people give you spoken instructions, can you remember them, or do you need to write them down? Do you like learning in laboratories where you get your hands on things, or do you prefer regular classes?

Then think about how you learn things on your own, when pursuing your hobbies, for instance. What role do books play in your learning? hands-on experience? spoken information? learning from other people?

You probably won't come up with any firm conclusions in this **Quest.** In fact, you may discover that at different times, you have different ways of learning. If you do, that's all to the good, because the more ways you have to learn, the more likely it is you will find answers to your questions. In your Learner's Notebook write down your observations.

For those of you who are *visual* learners, this pattern is displayed in Figure 1-2. A **Quest** begins when you have a question you want to answer. Perhaps it is a simple question, but it may also be very complicated with a number of parts to it. (More about that in the next chapter.) When you have zeroed in on the question(s) you want to answer, start looking for resources—materials to supply answers. These resources can include people as well as books and can even lead you into designing some experiments and research on your own.

As you collect information, you will sift through it and analyze it, looking for answers. Sometimes you will follow the "scientific method" of inquiry, studying data to see whether or not your "hypothesis" or educated guess is correct. (More about that in Chapter 7.) At other times, you will simply be comparing what you've read in books to what people have told you. Eventually, you will come to some conclusions about your question, and at that point, I hope, you're ready to share your information with other people.

By the way, the **Quest** design in Figure 1-2 is patterned after something called a compass rose, which sailors use to show all the possible "points" or directions in which their ship might sail. The compass rose is to remind you to keep looking in new directions in learning. Don't always head off the same old way into the sunset.

Please remember, too, that this is just a *schematic* or rough picture of the learning process. You'll figure out the best ways of proceeding for yourself.

Each of these stages or steps will be discussed in its own place in the book. For the rest of this chapter, I want to explore some topics you might consider to begin **Questing.**

Getting Started

What *ideas* interest and excite you? That is what **Questing** is all about.

You can begin a **Quest** any time you have a question, and it can continue as long as you remain curious. A **Quest** can take just a few minutes to complete (like finding out who won the 1960 World Series) or it can go on for a lifetime (as in learning how to play a musical instrument to the best of your ability).

As an example of how you might begin, let's start with *advertising:* Do you find yourself bombarded with TV, radio, and magazine ads every day? Do you think ads are silly or effective? Did you know that advertisers spend millions and millions of dollars every year trying to reach the pre-teen and teen markets? Perhaps you could **Quest** into advertising and learn more about how it influences your life.

FIGURE 1-2: The Quest Design

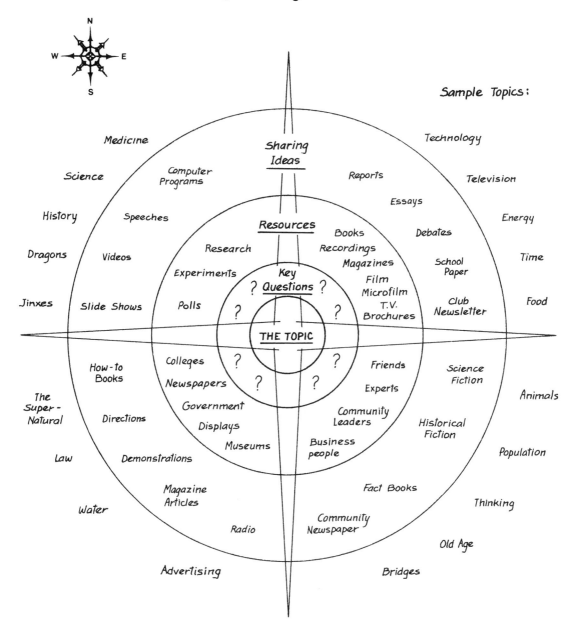

* * * QUESTING * * *

Consider the following list of ideas as starting points for **Quests.**
In your notebook free-associate on topics that catch your imagination. Just write down whatever comes into your mind. You
don't need to write something for every topic, just the ones that
make sense or hold interest for you.

Advertising	People and animals	Baseball
Technology	Blood	Weather
Energy	Sugar	Jokes
Jinxes	Pianos	Stars
Measurement	Fasteners	Furniture
Light	Autos	Things that glow
Electricity	Knighthood	Loans
Ponies	Pigs	Cats
Flowers	Fruits	Roots
Leaves	Twigs	Rocks
Marriage	Video	Tires
Bridges	Cameras	Books
Buses	Flight	Dragons
Yesterday	Today	Tomorrow

Or consider *people and animals.* How are animals part of your life?
Do you have pets? How do they bring pleasure to you? Think of how
other animals may be part of your life as food! Or as a source of
clothing. Or as a source of entertainment (as in circuses). How long
has humankind been using animals for its own benefit? Have you
read or heard anything about the use of animals for scientific experiments? Do you know anything about attempts to prevent cruelty to
animals?

Baseball is called the great American pastime. Whether or not you play baseball or softball you might consider looking into the legends and lore of the game, studying its history (Did Abner Doubleday really invent the game?), its records (Who is the all-time strike-out king as a pitcher? as a batter?), or even the coming season (Who are the best bets to win the American and National league pennants?).

You may want to look into the idea of *technology* (Where is so-called high tech taking us? What will the future hold for high-tech computers? for high-tech weapons?).

Have you ever wondered what's in *blood* (What chemicals does it contain? How does its flow control our lives?).

You could examine that perpetual topic of conversation, the *weather* (Did you know that for just a few dollars you can construct a weather station to create your own forecasts?).

You can **Quest** into *bridges* (from bridges between teeth to river spanners), *pigs* (from baby piglets to sausages), *video* (from TV situation comedies to rock 'n' roll tapes), *flight* (from birds to supersonic

---

✳ ✳ ✳ QUESTING ✳ ✳ ✳

In your Learner's Notebook set aside a section titled **Quest** Ideas. Begin making a list of the things that interest you most in life. You can list these as one-word topics:

Spiders

or, perhaps better, ask some questions:

What are cobwebs made of?

Free-associate from one idea to another. For example, *Jinxes* might get you thinking of *Superstitions* which could lead you to *The Supernatural* which could carry you on to the *Twilight Zone*. From *Twigs* you might go to *Trees* to *Lumber* to *Construction* to *Architecture* to *Drafting*. Keep adding to your notebook regularly, and soon you'll have a storehouse of **Quest** ideas, even if you can't investigate all of them right now.

planes), and the *past, present,* and *future* (from yesterday's history to today's problems to predictions about tomorrow).

You might **Quest** into *dragons* (whole books have been written speculating about whether or not mythical dragons could fly). Or you could look into *things that glow* (from fireflies to radium watch dials to fluorescent lights).

There are many places to get ideas for **Quests.** A good way to find them is to browse through newspapers and magazines for subjects that look interesting. Another good place is the library. I like to spend time just scanning the card catalog or the bookshelves looking for ideas that pique my curiosity.

You can find **Quest** ideas in school as you are reading your text-books: Just jot down questions that occur to you as you study. If you ever get frustrated by some schoolwork—just can't seem to get the hang of it—you can put down some questions in your Learner's Notebook and do some research at a later point. Even though most learning **Quests** can be "fun," some of them can begin with issues or problems that don't, at first glance, seem to be all that pleasurable. So if science or math or history is proving troublesome, it may be that a **Quest** is just what you need to find where you are going.

Add to your lists as you listen to the radio and as you talk with friends. Do grownups ever puzzle you? Plan to **Quest** about *adults.* Do younger brothers and sisters drive you crazy? Put down *kids* as an idea for exploration. (Maybe you can do some reading that will help you understand just *why* brothers and sisters haven't gotten along from at least the time the Biblical Cain slew his brother Abel.)

There is literally no limit to the kind and number of topics you can choose for **Quests.** Once you've prepared a basic list and start seeking answers to questions, you'll probably find topics for **Quests** popping into your head at odd times of the day (and night). I like to carry around a small pocket pad just for jotting down ideas and inspirations at the moment they come into my head.

* * * QUESTING * * *

More Topics for **Quests**

Dreams	Visions	Nightmares
Tobacco	China	Wilderness
Optical illusions	General illusions	Testing
Hawaii	Fiji	Australia
Success	Transplants	Bionics
Elections	Leadership	Chairs
Tools	Stock market	Safety
Pedigree dogs	Mutts	Animal training
Telephones	Diamonds	Churches
Manners	Europe	X-rays
Saving	Conserving	Hoarding
Teddy bears	Frontiers	Breakthroughs
Muscles	Bones	Nerves
Extrasensory perception	Intelligence Quotient (I.Q.)	

* * * QUESTING * * *

Still More Topics for Quests

Europe	Religion	Eagles
Trees	Gardens	Architecture
Ponds	Age	Death
Bonsai	Spices	Antiques
Spring	Fall	Winter
Summer	Junk	Miniatures
Dollhouses	Model railroads	Go-carts
Heat	Cold	Swimming
Horses	Jackpots	Violence
Gambling	Language	Counting
Competition	Games	Careers
Sewers	Psychology	Elephants

2 The Art of Questioning

"Good questions outrank easy answers," says Paul A. Samuelson (*Newsweek,* August 21, 1978, Lewis, p. 70). Although most of us want *answers* when we come up against problems and difficulties, the phrasing of good questions is equally important. There are times when an imaginative thinker may want to step back for a moment and say, not, "What is the answer?" but "What was the question in the first place?"

It is important to separate trivial from important questions. Most of us enjoy answering trivia questions, showing off the depths of our knowledge. I'm a modest trivia expert on soft drinks and can answer your questions about the inventor of Coca-Cola (Dr. John Pemberton, Atlanta, Georgia, 1886) or Pepsi-Cola (Caleb Bradham, New Berne, North Carolina, 1890) or why there's no period in Dr Pepper (advertising people thought it cluttered up the logotype). Other people I know are trivia experts on sports or music and can answer questions on everything from who won the 1919 World Series to the number of symphonies composed by Wolfgang Amadeus Mozart. Still others have incredible knowledge of automobiles (When were

Studebakers last made in this country?) or government (How many representatives does California have?) or finances (What was the gross national product last year?). One fellow I know even makes money as the trivia expert at a local restaurant; he specializes in stumping the audience with questions on odd facts.

Test yourself. Can you answer the following questions?

Who was the oldest bridegroom in history?
What language has the most vowels?
How big was the largest snowflake ever measured?

The answers are taken from Bruce Witherspoon's *The Second Mammoth Book of Trivia.*

"Ralph Cambridge . . . was 105 years old when he married Mrs. Adriana Kapp, age 70, in South Africa in September of 1971" (p. 323).

"A Vietnamese language called Sedang can claim the most vowel sounds, 55" (p. 411).

"The largest snowflake on record measured eight inches in width" (p. 442).

If you couldn't answer those questions, don't feel bad. There doesn't seem to be any good reason for carrying those kinds of answers around in your head. That's what books are for, among other things—to store knowledge that doesn't need to be maintained in your memory banks.

One could ask an infinite number of trivia questions. You could ask, "What's the longest tunnel on earth?" or "What's the smallest dog?" or "What's the only Great Lake that lies entirely within the United States?" You might want to ask "How many ribs do people have?" or "How many books are stored in the Library of Congress?" or "How much chewing gum is consumed around the world each day?"

Such questions are fun to try to answer (and to look up). I'm not going to tell you the answers to the questions above, but you could find them in Bruce Witherspoon's book or in any number of references in your library. (See Chapter 4 for more ideas on information sources.)

However, one should ask whether these are *important* questions. Does it matter if you know who the oldest bridegroom was? So what if you know that Lake Michigan is the only lake that is entirely within the United States? (Oops! I just gave you one of the answers.)

My point is not to make light of trivia games and questions. But *trivia* is, to quote Webster's *Collegiate* dictionary, "commonplace, ordinary, of little worth or importance."

There are more important questions to be asked.

✳ ✳ ✳ QUESTING ✳ ✳ ✳

In recent years the game Trivial Pursuit has been very popular. It involves testing your knowledge of trivial information, and it's fun to play if you take it in the right spirit. There have also been some spinoffs from Trivial Pursuit, games developed about particular sports teams or about food or even about towns or communities. You might enjoy:

Playing Trivial Pursuit (you can find it in most gift or stationery stores that sell games)

Playing one of the spinoff games (you'll find those at the game shop, too)

Inventing your own trivia game, say, about your home town or about your school. When was your town settled? by whom? How many people first lived there? Who was the first mayor? When was the first school built? When was your school built? How many kids go there? Who was the first principal? What are the school sports records? What famous or almost famous people have graduated from your school?

Playing these sorts of games can be challenging and enjoyable, but keep in mind that the questions being asked and answered are not always important ones.

The Questions Worth Asking

Neil Postman and Charles Weingartner have argued that good learners:
  · have confidence in their ability to learn.
  · enjoy solving problems.
  · prefer to rely on their own judgment.
  · are usually not fearful of being wrong.
  · are emphatically not fast answerers.
  · are flexible.
  · have a high degree of respect for facts (pp. 31-32).
Good learners will naturally know a lot (or know how to find out information—the facts) and will "respect" the way factual information helps make them reach sound decisions. Good learners may even be able to play trivia games quite successfully, because in the course of their learning they have accumulated a good deal of factual information.

More important, however, is that good learners have *inquiring* and *independent* minds. They are flexible, meaning that they can listen to and evaluate a variety of opinions while preparing to make their own judgments.

Not pointed out on Postman and Weingartner's list is the fact that good learners are also *good questioners*. Someone once said, "There are things that are known and things that are unknown; in between are doors" (Lewis, p. 142). Questions often prove to be the doors, or, perhaps more accurately, the *keys* that can unlock the doors, to the unknown.

Having read about the importance of question asking, you can probably figure out why the central process of learning in *The Young Learner's Handbook* is called **Quest**ing. A good **Quest** begins with a set of good questions, pure and simple.

There is no way that any book or any teacher can actually *make* you a better question-asker than you already are. No magic formula for asking questions will produce flawless ones; no supercomputer

---

* * * QUESTING * * *

Look through the list of traits of good learners. In your note-book, write a self-assessment about your own learning habits. Don't feel guilty if you don't have all those characteristics; after all, Neil Postman and Charles Weingartner are describing a kind of *ideal* learner. If there are areas where you think you need practice, you can use the rest of this chapter on question asking to help develop your skills.

---

can think up better questions than human beings can ask. However, as Allen Harrison and Robert M. Bramson have suggested in their book, *Styles of Thinking,* "Most people, most of the time, think about things in only one way. Some people occasionally use two ways of thinking. Very few people ever approach a situation in more than two ways" (p. 1). By consciously **Questing** in new directions, you can strengthen those skills. You can stretch out, pushing your mind to the limits, exploring all the ideas that potentially interest you.

---

* * * QUESTING * * *

Some questions that interest me are shown in Figure 2-1. Your own questions will be much more interesting to you. Start a page of your Learner's Notebook that is simply labeled *Questions.* Begin using this page to list questions you think would be interesting to answer. Some of the questions may be of the trivial sort; most will be more important. You might use as-terisks to denote those that you think are especially important. Add to the list as you become more and more skilled at ques-tioning and **Questing.**

FIGURE 2-1:   Some Questions to Explore

On Europe. How old is Europe? What are its boundaries? When was it first settled? How is it changing today? When was it last at war? How well do Europeans get along with one another?

On Eagles. How many eagles are still alive? Where do they live? What do they eat? Are they endangered? Why was the eagle selected as our national bird?

On Trees. How many different kinds of trees are there? How many different kinds grow near where I live? How do trees grow? How old do they become? Where are the biggest trees? What are the smallest trees? Are trees expanding or diminishing in number and kind?

On Age. How long am I likely to live? Who are the oldest people? What are the secrets of their survival? How are elderly people taken care of? What do I need to do to protect myself for my own old age?

On Religion. How many different religions are there in the world? How many people in the world do *not* follow a religion? How do various religions differ in what they believe? What beliefs do they hold in common? Which religions are growing? Which are shrinking in numbers?

On Careers. What kinds of jobs are open to a person with my interests and abilities? How can one best choose a career or job? Can you change jobs later if you find out that you're not happy? What kind of help is available to a person interested in choosing or changing a career?

Ballooning Your Way to Good Questions

You've blown up a good many balloons in your lifetime. You start with something small and lifeless (somebody once described an empty balloon as looking like a toad skin before somebody put the toad inside). As you pump in air, the balloon grows and swells. Ballooning is a technique for developing questions that lets you link your questions to one another, expanding as you pump in ideas. A schematic or visual representation of ballooning is shown in Figure 2-2.

FIGURE 2-2: Ballooning

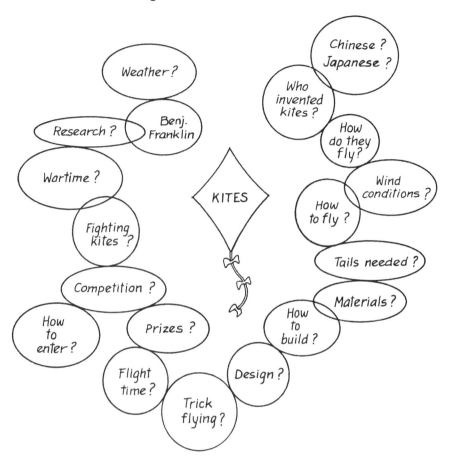

The balloons are a little like the "Venn diagrams" you may have encountered in mathematics class, showing that questions overlap with one another, just as some mathematical sets overlap. (If you haven't studied Venn diagrams, don't worry about it. Add a question in your notebook: "What's a Venn diagram?") In ballooning for ideas, you start with a central idea or question, then see just how many interesting connections you can make. Each new question goes into a new balloon that overlaps more or less with its pals.

You begin with an idea that's been on your mind, a topic that you are interested in. Then you begin writing down questions. For example, I'll take a topic from a newspaper article that just caught my eye. The topic is kites. At first you might not think there's much to kites— just pieces of flying paper or plastic. You might think that questions about kites would be trivial. However, if I tell you that the sale of kites has become a $100-million-dollar-a-year industry in this country, you'll realize that on kites hang a tale of some interest and possible significance. *Kites,* then, is written at the center of our balloon in Figure 2-2.

Then I start asking questions, "ballooning" out from the center. One of my questions would simply be "Who invented kites?" I seem to recall that the Chinese or the Japanese were early fliers of kites, so I draw a balloon out from the "invention" question.

Most of us have heard that Benjamin Franklin flew a kite in a lightning storm to "discover" electricity. I wonder whether that is legend or fact, so I create a balloon simply labeled, "Benj. Franklin." However, that balloon leads me to other questions. Have kites ever been used in other kinds of research—say, for weather?

I also wonder about the uses of kites in wartime, because it seems to me I read or heard someplace that kites were flown over enemy lines in World War II, and I can remember as a youngster seeing a neighbor's kite, decorated like an airplane with a bull's-eye painted on it, that had been used by the military for target practice.

From the military uses of kites, my questions drift to fighting kites, which I've seen on TV, and that, in turn, opens up another whole avenue of exploration about kite competitions. Are there kite contests in my area? What do they give prizes for? Are there prizes for design? For highest flying? Trick flying? Flying more than one kite at a time? How do I enter kite contests?

We've all seen the trouble Charlie Brown has flying kites in Charles Schulz's *Peanuts* strip. I wonder about techniques and strategies for flying kites. Do kites need tails? What kind of wind conditions are best for kite flying? Is it dangerous to fly a kite in a rainstorm?

Another set of balloons contains my questions about kite design. How many different kinds of kites are there? What do they look like? How do they differ in form and function?

And a whole set of questions comes to mind about just plain kite building. How easy or difficult is it to build one's own kite? What materials can you use? Where can you get designs for kites? If you get good enough, can you design your own? As Figure 2-2 shows, pretty soon you have a whole page of balloons depicting your questions.

✳ ✳ ✳ COMPUTERQUEST ✳ ✳ ✳

A computer word-processing program is another good way to keep track of questions you have, because the program allows you to add new questions at any point. You might start a word processing file simply labeled:

KITES

Then you could add some questions or words associated with it:

Inventors   Uses   Making

Then, as more and more ideas occurred to you, you could add more questions.

Chinese?   War?   Materials?
Japanese?   Research?   Plastic? Paper?

Still later, you could add new categories of questions or enlarge on some of the ones you already have:

Inventors
Were kites a Japanese or Chinese invention?
Have Americans invented any interesting kites?
Can you patent a kite design?

With word processing, you can keep adding ideas without having to recopy your page. There are also some computer programs designed to help you develop and organize your questions. Ask at your computer store about programs called "idea processors."

Brainstorming for Ideas and Questions

You'll probably surprise yourself on many occasions as you are doing a balloon diagram; you'll discover that you have many more questions on a topic than you imagined.

Still, if one mind is fertile, two or more minds are fertilizer. If you collaborate with one or more friends, you can come up with an astonishing list of ideas. **Questing** works every bit as well with a group of people as it does as a solo activity. A technique known as "brainstorming" may prove helpful.

Researchers in the field of communications discovered long ago that in group discussions, people often are quite negative toward one another's ideas. As soon as somebody proposes an idea, somebody else objects to it or says it's a bad one. You've probably had a similar experience with friends. "Whaddya wanna do today?" somebody asks, and no matter what suggestion comes up, other people object, "Ah, that's no fun; I don't wanna do that." The result is not very productive.

Brainstorming operates on the principle that a group of people should create a number of ideas first, then go back and criticize or evaluate. In terms of developing good questions, the procedure works this way:

One, get an interested group of people together to brainstorm about a particular subject, say, kites or sports or a school problem. Almost any topic will work.

Two, appoint one person as recorder or secretary—somebody who can write clearly and rapidly.

Three, get a large sheet of paper and fasten it on the wall. Or use a chalk board.

Four, start raising questions. The secretary can write them in balloons as we've seen in Figure 2-2, or you can simply have him or her list the questions in columns.

Five, do *not* criticize. It is out of order to say, "That's a great question" or "That's a lousy one." Concentrate only on raising questions.

Six, encourage people to "coattail" on one anothers' question. That is, if the person next to you says something that triggers ideas in your mind, it's perfectly acceptable for you to build on that idea and turn it into a question of your own.

Seven, set a time limit of, say, ten to fifteen minutes. See how many questions you and your friends can raise.

Brainstorming *works.* You'll be amazed at just how many different questions you can come up with if you follow the rules, yet use your full imagination.

✳ ✳ ✳ QUESTING ✳ ✳ ✳

Here are some topics that might be interesting to you and/or your friends. Try ballooning or brainstorming for interesting questions on:

Radar	Smoking	Stars
Tigers	Rain	Crowns
Martial arts	Lizards	Astrology
Awards	Royalty	Satellites
Pumping iron	Vitamins	Codes
Machines	Russia	The Pentagon
Triangles	Squares	Circles

Lateral Thinking

Edward DeBono says that people often get set in their patterns and always follow a straight or obvious line of thought. In his book, *Lateral* (or "sideways") *Thinking,* DeBono argues that we need to see topics in new ways. Here are some ways to improve your own "lateral thinking."

Think of *parallels* and *similarities*. (How is a kite like a balloon? What can you do with kites that you can't do with balloons? How are kites like airplanes? Can we learn anything about airplanes from kites? Can we learn anything about kites from airplanes?)

Think of *opposites*. (How is a kite like a submarine, something that goes down rather than up? Has anybody ever flown a kite from a submarine? Could kites be used as some sort of signaling system in submarines when radio silence has been imposed?)

Think in *metaphors* or *comparisons*. (How is a kite like a bird? like a butterfly on the wing? like an eagle soaring? like a planet in the sky? like a space satellite?)

Think of *applications*. (How can we use kites for more than fun? Could kites be used as a communications system? How could they be used to predict the weather or to learn more about electricity? Can you use a kite as a super radio antenna?)

Think of the *future*. (What does the future hold for kites? What sorts of space-age materials might be used in kite construction? Will kids still fly kites one hundred years from now? What might those kites look like? Will you teach your children to fly kites?)

Think just plain *wacky*. (Could we invent a stringless kite? Could you build a kite big enough to carry a person? Could a kite be wired with a TV camera to provide surveillance? What about a kite to scare crows from a cornfield?)

Growing Big Questions from Little Ones

Ideas like ballooning, brainstorming, and lateral thinking are designed to help you create as many questions as you can. There comes a time, however, when it is important to provide some focus, just to make certain your questions are not running off in all directions.

As I look at Figure 2-2, I see one whole set of questions connected together in the general area of *applications* (What can you *do* with kites?). Another set is related to *flight* (How do kites fly and in what ways is this like airplane or bird flight?). A third area is *design* (How do you make and fly kites?). And a fourth topic is *contests* or *competition* (If I get good at kite flying or building, can I test my

*** * * * QUESTING * * ***

Here are still more ideas for exploration. Do you have any interest in any of them? Pick one or two and try out the idea of lateral thinking. Write questions about the topic based on opposites, parallels and similarities, metaphors, applications, and the future. Then just go wacky and think of all the possibilities:

Monuments	Brothers/sisters	Banjos
Fur	Weight loss	Terrorism
Parents	Turtles	Shells
Classifications	Circuses	Growing old
Movies	Comets	Sportsmanship
Cheating	Revenge	Ballpoint pens
Antarctic	Save the whales	Bugs
Glass	Plastic	Hats

skills against those of other people?). In a sense, then, I have pulled together all my smaller questions into "superquestions" to guide my learning. You can do this for yourself simply by drawing dotted lines around the parts of your balloon diagram (as I've done in Figure 2-3), but if the page gets too cluttered, you may want to draw a new diagram on a fresh sheet of paper. (One of the advantages of using a computer for question asking is that you can insert the superquestions any place you want, without recopying.)

How you pull things together will vary with the kinds of questions you want to answer. If you're just out to build and fly a kite, you might ask a question or two and then head off to the library (or a store that sells kites) to find some plans and materials. On the other hand, if you are doing a report for school, you might want to develop all the balloon questions you can think of and then use your "superquestions" as subheads within your report.

Remember that I'm only suggesting guidelines to help you channel

FIGURE 2-3: Superquestions

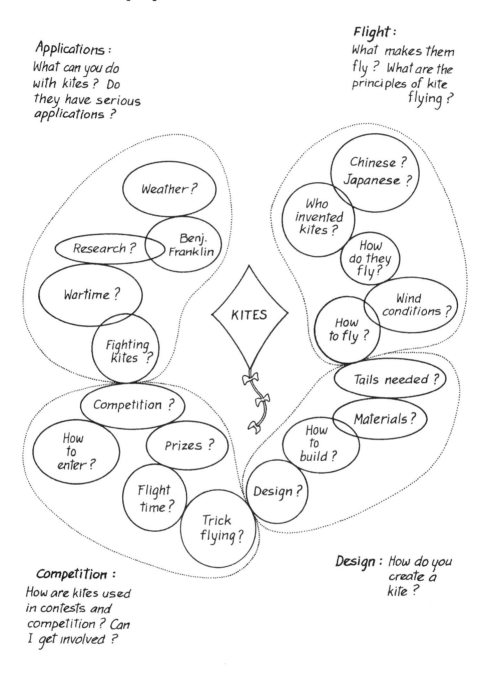

Applications :
What can you do
with kites ? Do
they have serious
applications ?

Flight :
What makes them
fly ? What are the
principles of kite
flying ?

Weather ?

Research ?

Benj.
Franklin

Wartime ?

Fighting
kites ?

Chinese ?
Japanese ?

Who
invented
kites ?

How
do they
fly ?

Wind
conditions ?

KITES

How
to fly ?

Competition ?

How
to
enter ?

Prizes ?

Flight
time ?

Trick
flying ?

Design ?

How
to
build ?

Tails needed ?

Materials ?

Competition :
How are kites used
in contests and
competition ? Can
I get involved ?

Design : How do you
create a
kite ?

and organize the creativity that is within you. The essential point is that in learning on your own, you need first to see all the possibilities through good questions, then to focus your study, knowing that you probably don't have the time or the energy to answer all the questions you create.

About **Unanswered** *Questions*

It is important to note that *not all the questions you ask will have answers!* There are some questions that just don't have answers (yet). Sometimes an unanswered question simply means that some research needs to be done, and I will take up that topic in Chapter 7.

However, to show you that even professional question-askers and answerers sometimes run up against walls, you'll be interested in knowing that scientists also have identified what they call some "world enigmas," puzzles which research and creative thinking have failed to answer *and which never may be answered.* Here, then, are some world championship unanswered questions:

What is the nature of matter? We know a great deal about the structure of molecules and atoms, but in the end, the nature or the "stuff" of the universe remains a mystery. We just don't know what the world is made of. A related, unanswered (and possibly unanswerable) question is, "What's the smallest particle in the universe?" Scientists keep finding smaller and smaller elements in nature. There seems to be no end, and it may be that the smallest particle may never be found.

What is the origin of life? Most religions have an answer to that question. The Bible, for example, says that on the sixth day of the creation of the universe, God created man. Still, science has yet to figure out precisely how that spark of life came about and what exactly happened to turn objects into living creatures. We know that at some point, eons ago, tiny organisms came into life, but how? There are several different theories, but no one of them will probably ever be proven absolutely correct.

What is the arrangement of nature? If you look into many science textbooks, you see that information is neatly laid out by chapters, which suggests that we know just how the universe is put together. But in fact every time scientists have created a system for classifying the animals, vegetables, and minerals on this planet, they find exceptions: animals that don't seem to fit any category, plants or rocks that "don't belong." All this is another way of saying that science has not yet figured out all the answers.

What is thinking? We human beings are conscious creatures, aware of what's going on around us, perceiving the world, thinking about it, making decisions. Science knows a fair amount about how the brain works, how three and a half pounds of cells receives and sends messages that control our reactions, yet, there's still no explanation of what makes all the parts of the brain work together to function as a conscious whole. (Some religions offer an answer to this enigma and say that consciousness is a result of a human being's soul.)

---

* * * QUESTING * * *

There are other questions that fascinate and perplex people, questions that seem to have no answers—questions about life and death and thinking and love and hate and wars. You undoubtedly have some questions that puzzle you, too, questions about your relationships with other people, questions about the significance of your own life, questions about the lives and deaths of people (and animals) around you. You might set aside a page in your Learner's Handbook that you call *Puzzles and Enigmas.* Use that as a place to write down your questions about some of the mysteries of life. You may not find answers easily, but simply writing down the questions will help you clarify them in your own mind.

More Questions to Answer

Most of the questions that you pose *do* have answers, or *tentative* or *partial* answers. (It's important never to think that one has found the all-time, permanent, unchangeable answer to *anything*.) To conclude this chapter, I will simply list some more questions that I find interesting. If any of these intrigue you, you're welcome to them. Just start creating a set of balloons as we did for "kites" earlier in the chapter. Then read on; in the next several chapters I'll get into specifics about how to find some answers.

✳ ✳ ✳ QUESTING ✳ ✳ ✳

More Questions to Answer

· How does life in Canada differ from that in the United States?

· How many farms are there? How has farming changed in the past several decades? How will the food of the future be grown?

· Where did the games of chess and checkers come from? Who plays these games? How do computerized chess and checkers games work?

· Will computers ever be able to think like people?

· How much money is being spent on video games? Who plays these games? Are they good or bad for you?

· Who invented "rock 'n' roll"?

· How does country and western differ from other kinds of music?

· Why do people gamble? What is the appeal of gambling? What kinds of legal and illegal gambling goes on in this country?

· Can psychologists really figure out what's going on in your mind? Do lie detectors work? Will there ever be a computer that can read your mind?

(Continued)

(*Continued*)

· Are there ghosts?

· Why do people, especially young people, kill themselves?

· How soon do babies start learning? Do babies learn anything while still inside the mother?

· What is life like for a police officer?

· How many different kinds of sports are played around the world? Why do people like to play competitive games?

· How do losers feel about themselves?

· How many different kinds of shoes are there? Will shoelaces ever go out of use?

· How do vacuum cleaners work?

· Is there any point in developing bigger and better weapons?

· What is life like for a superstar?

· How do computer chips work?

· Why are clarinets so complicated?

· Do plants really respond to human voices?

· Why are cats so independent?

· What's in breakfast cereal?

· How much money do people put on charge cards?

· What will we do when the sources of crude oil run out?

3 Data Gathering

The high school I attended was built about 1900, and its architecture followed classical design, with huge columns on all sides of the building.* Warriors and maidens were sculpted into the building near the roof line, and mottos and slogans were carved in cement (which would, in ancient times, have been marble). Above the main entrance to the school was written the phrase, "Knowledge is power." (Actually, it was carved in Roman letters in which *w*'s looked like *v*'s, so it said, "Knovledge is pover," much to the amazement and amusement of us kids.) Beside that slogan were two figures, one a warrior putting down his shield and spear, the other a bearded man in long robes reading a book. We eventually figured out that the people who had designed the school were trying to tell us that *learning* was better than fighting, something that I came to believe and believe to this day.

---

*This same high school building was once featured in Ripley's *Believe It or Not.* The school was built on a hill, and the street wound around it in a horseshoe shape, giving it street level entrances on the first, second, and third floors. Mr. Ripley said this was a unique building, believe it or not!

35

A lesson I learned less successfully in high school was how to keep good records of my learning. "Take careful notes," my high school teachers kept telling me, but try as I would, I never seemed to learn how. My notebooks were filled with sketches and doodles and jottings to my friends, but not with very good or even *readable* notes. In my junior year we were assigned a research paper and were taught how to keep notes on file cards. I tried my best, but somehow my file cards always turned out like my notes—scrawled illegibly and placed in some sort of order whose plan I couldn't remember afterward. I had a very difficult time writing my paper, because I couldn't find notes on half the stuff I had read.

Now, I have a pretty good memory, so in high school I could usually get away with poor notes. In college it became necessary to become a better notetaker, though it was a real struggle, and now that I'm a writer and teacher, I work hard to keep careful records and notes on what I read and see. I wish now I could send word back to those high school teachers who tried so hard to make a notewriter of me and say, "You were right!" Knovledge *is* pover, but good notes and records are power, too.

I have also learned as a writer and teacher that notetaking is just the tip of a much larger iceberg that I am calling data gathering. In our world today knowledge still is power, but as Irwin Blue says, "*Information* equals power" (italics added, Lewis, p. 132). And, as B. C. Forbes adds, "*Information* means money" (italics added, Lewis, p. 132). I'm not claiming that good data gathering will make you rich. However, what these two people are suggesting is that the more information you have at your disposal, the better your position in making important decisions.

In fact, these days *information* has become a kind of "cash crop." An entire industry of data gathering and rapid communications has developed. There are people who make their lives as researchers, digging out information that is needed in business, and fortunes are spent on bigger, better, faster computers and telecommunications systems so information can be transferred rapidly and in huge volumes.

Scholars today talk about the knowledge *explosion.* There is so much research and learning going on in the world that people have difficulty keeping up to date in their fields. Librarians are struggling to get all the new material stored away on the shelves, and technology is increasingly playing a role in how information is sorted.

Sometimes understanding comes to a person through insight and intuition, as in the old cartoon stereotype of a light bulb switching on in the brain. However, an enormous amount of learning grows, not from magical moments of genius, but from people studying the information they have available, or, in computer jargon, studying the *database* from which they operate. Industries vie with each other to create large databases so that they will have the competitive edge in the "information equals money" game.

Each of us also has a personal "database." This includes all the information we store in our heads, plus the resources, tools, and information we keep close at hand—books, telephones, computers.

I'm *not* going to try to persuade you just to "take good notes" in this chapter (although that *is* good advice). Just as I had to learn the value of good record keeping myself, you'll have to figure out what works for you. Thus I will not only discuss notes and notetaking, but the whole iceberg of data gathering, suggesting some of the ways in which you can save information and ideas to put them to use in your learning.

Knowledge, after all, really *is* power.

Collections: Saving the Real Thing

Museum curators save *artifacts,* objects that tell something about the age in which they were made. A million-year-old rock has a story inside it, a story about the formation of the earth. An antique car from the 1930s has a number of stories attached to it: stories about the materials in the car and how they were shaped, stories about fashion and style and what people wanted an automobile to be like in the thirties. Collections of stuffed birds tell stories of wildlife in a particular place; toy and game exhibits tell tales about the lives of

both children and grownups. Even today our society is creating artifacts—the toys you played with as a child may be antique "collectibles" in twenty-five or thirty years. Museum curators save these
artifacts as a useful way to study the world.

In one sense, collecting objects or artifacts is even better than taking notes as a way of data gathering, because collecting allows you to
work with the real thing.

The chances are that you're a "curator" already. Perhaps you collect rocks or save photos of rock stars; possibly you hoard stamps,
dolls, cans and bottles, banners, T-shirts, posters, or souvenirs from
places you've visited. Aside from the pleasure of collecting these
things, your collection can serve as a way for you to learn more about
people and the world they live in.

However, if your collections are anything like mine were as a
youngster (I collected pennants, stamps, and Boy Scout patches),
they're stuffed in a drawer somewhere with parts and pieces all in a
tangle. (If you're getting the impression from this chapter that I was a
messy kid, you're right.) To get the most *learning* from your collection (and to share your information with other people), it's useful to
organize it.

Museum curators gather material not just to have it on hand, but
to *interpret* it. Fred Schroeder, a professor at the University of Min-
nesota, Duluth, says that ideally, the objects in a well-planned museum collection "speak their messages clearly" (Schroeder, p. 1).
That is, a museum collection will be arranged so that casual viewers
can figure out the significance for themselves. People need help understanding the full meaning of the objects they see in a museum,
whether stuffed buffalo or weapons from thousands of years ago. He
suggests a number of questions that museum curators (and young
learners) can ask about the things they collect. You might want to
apply some of these questions, adapted from Professor Schroeder's
list of "Seven Ways to Look at an Artifact," to your own collections:

How are or were these items used by people? What signs of wear
and tear do you see? How have the objects you collect changed "over
time," that is, what are the differences among older and newer items

in your collection? Can you see any differences in style? What seem to be the trends?

To make that more concrete: if you collect American commemorative stamps, you can compare them—big ones, little ones, colorful ones, plain ones. What differences do you see? How do older stamps differ from newer ones? Can you see trends in the subjects for commemorative stamps or the kind of artwork on them? If your stamps are canceled, you can think about the cities from which they were mailed and consider how the stamps helped people communicate. If you have stamps from other countries, you can make comparisons and try to figure out why U.S. stamps look different from those of, say, an African or Far Eastern country.

That knowledge, in turn, can help you *organize* your collection in interesting ways, perhaps grouping stamps by subjects or time period or some other characteristic that you've decided is important.

✻ ✻ ✻ QUESTING ✻ ✻ ✻

Take a critical look at your collections. Could they use some organizing? Could you *learn* more about a collection by organizing it or reorganizing it? Museum curators are quite interested in how to display their collections so other people can enjoy and learn from them. How could your collections best be arranged or displayed? If you've constructed a learning center as suggested in Chapter 1, you might want to use a portion of that space to serve as a museum. Also check an office supply store or hobby shop for folders, files, and even cases that might be useful in getting your collection organized. Or talk to other people who collect and see what they've done by way of mounting and displaying the objects they've saved over the years.

In addition to thinking about your existing collections, you might be interested in launching some new ones as part of a learning **Quest.** If you became intrigued by kites from our discussion in the previous chapter, you might begin saving kites, either unusual ones you find in stores or ones you design and create yourself. If you are studying a problem in the world today, you could create a clipping file of newspaper articles.

You might also want to become your family *archivist* or collector of memories. Museums today are particularly interested in family history, the record of how just plain folks lived, people who were *not* generals or presidents or famous inventors. Unfortunately, often important family records and artifacts are lost over time. As your family's archivist you could be certain that twenty years from now, when people want to remember what your family was like "way back when," they'll have the materials available.

The Paper Chase

In the history of humankind, writing developed very slowly. At first, it was a slow and laborious process, as people carved or embossed letters in clay or stone. Not only was this slow, it was inconvenient and made writing impractical. Egyptian *papyrus,* a form of paper first created from fibers of the papyrus plant about three thousand years ago, made writing a bit more convenient. However, papyrus was expensive, so that only the wealthy made much use of it. The Chinese are credited with making the first true paper about two thousand years ago, but paper remained expensive, and writing was a skill mastered by very few people. It wasn't until the 1800s that manufacturing processes made paper truly inexpensive, and since then its low cost and availability has put writing and books and newspapers into the hands of anyone who is interested in becoming literate. Today we don't hesitate to use paper freely for everything from notes to friends to wrappings for junk food. Plain old paper, the stuff you reach for and crumple up and throw away, is remarkably plentiful and inexpensive.*

---

*One of the things I like about being a writer is the low cost of the "raw materials": the manuscript paper on which this book was first written cost well under $10. And paper itself is just a small part of the cost of the actual book.

---

* * * QUESTING * * *

If the idea of being the family archivist appeals to you, collect your family's artifacts and begin organizing some of the materials that have accumulated over the years. You might:
· organize the family photo album.
· collect letters, postcards, and holiday greetings that have been sent to the family.
· sort through souvenirs or collectibles that the family has gathered on trips.
· put identifying labels on the bottom of special gifts you've received—say, the vase that Uncle Fudd brought with him from Missouri.
· encourage your family members to write their "memoirs," stories about their childhood, stories about important times in their lives. (This is also a good project to do with a tape recorder, leading to a collection of cassettes, with "artifacts"—real voices—preserved on tape.)
· write or tape record your own autobiography.
· create a "family tree," showing all your relatives and recording important information about their dates of birth, marriage, death, children, and where they live now.

As a learner, you'll find hundreds of ways of using paper as a way of storing data.

Filing Systems

As you engage in learning **Quests,** you'll quickly find yourself in need of ways of storing the paper you collect. You can keep documents in "trapper" folders, filing cabinets or boxes, index card files, or in plain brown cardboard boxes, bags, or envelopes. Even as you start a **Quest,** you should probably give some thought to developing a filing system that will let you store the paper you collect. Some students I know actually use fruit baskets (the half-bushel size) when collecting materials for research. I've also known students who stored clippings and notes in wastebaskets (carefully labeled so the paper isn't tossed out or treated as trash). Some people like to file their papers in notebooks, and I know scholars who have literally hundreds of loose-leaf notebooks lined up on their shelves, all containing notes and documents of various kinds. Your learning center ought to be designed to make storage of your paper data easy.

Paper Artifacts

Clippings from newspapers and magazines are much like the physical artifacts I described in the previous section, providing a concrete account of current happenings. If you subscribe to magazines or buy and read them regularly, you might want to set up a file in your learning center. Some magazines advertise boxes or binders that hold a year's issues easily. However, you can find less expensive magazine files at an office supply store or, cheaper still, you can simply save boxes and cartons that are the right size (empty cereal boxes, with top and one narrow side cut off, make good magazine files). After a while, though, all those magazines take up considerable space, so you might prefer to start a clipping file. I'm a habitual newspaper clipper, and my shirt pockets are often filled with articles I find interesting. Later I take them home or to the office and tuck them away in file folders. For more than two years before I started this book I filled folders with odds and ends of articles that I thought would be helpful in writing *The Young Learner's Handbook*. Naturally, you should make certain the periodicals you are cutting are not going to be used by somebody else. Few things are more annoying than to pick up a magazine you want to read and to discover that somebody has clipped from it.

If you can't cut up a periodical but want to save an article, it is permissible to make photocopies of articles for your own "scholarly" use. It is *not* legal to make a number of copies to give or sell to other people, and it's not in the spirit of fair play to copy something specifically to avoid having to buy the whole book or magazine.

In any case, you'll find that over time your files will become filled with interesting bits of paper with news, announcements, and articles. I find it informative to flip through my clipping files to remember what I've saved, and I often come across materials I'd forgotten about that will prove useful in my work.

Notes and Journals

At least as important as saving paper artifacts, however, is creating some documents of your own, writing down ideas and information that you find important. Thomas Jefferson is well known as the man who wrote the Declaration of Independence. Less well known is the fact that Jefferson was a lifetime learner, a man who read and studied everything he found intriguing and who kept very careful and detailed notes on his observations. Although Jefferson only published a single book, *Notes on Virginia,* his many volumes of journals have allowed scholars to gain an insight into a man who studied philosophy, law, ethics (moral behavior), farming, and architecture. Jefferson's knowledge was so great that as a seventy-year-old man, he designed the buildings for the new University of Virginia and then prescribed the *curriculum*—the course of study and books that the students would be required to read (Lehman).

Although I wrote earlier in this chapter that I was a poor notetaker in school, I discovered later that part of my problem was that I never realized notes could be anything more than just copying down *facts.* In school and college, I simply became bored writing down facts and figures from books and lectures; my mind would wander, and then my notes would get sloppy or doodley. Taking notes should be much more than a way of preserving names and dates; it is a good way to *react* to the ideas and information you are studying.

Keeping a Journal or Daybook. Many writers and learners spend a bit of time each day writing down their thoughts and observations on what they've seen. A journal is more than just a daily record of happenings; your journal should be a *response* to what goes on around you. Your daybook can record not only what you observe, but what you think about what you see. You can record unanswered questions or list ideas for things you want to examine further. If you've been keeping the Learner's Notebook as I suggested in the introduction, you're already well on your way to this sort of journal or daybook.

Notes Plus. In *The Young Writer's Handbook,* Susan Tchudi and I describe what we call "active notetaking," in which you not only write down facts you want to remember, but put down your reactions as well. I now call this sort of writing "Notes Plus." One of my students introduced me to an interesting variation on Notes Plus when she used different colored pens in her notebook, with the basic facts she wanted to remember in blue and her own comments and reactions in green:

"This is an amazing idea," she would write in green. Or, "I don't think there's enough evidence to support this." At one point she wrote, "You're telling me something different than what my other teachers are saying," which means that she was thinking critically about what she was being told. "I'll have to figure this out for myself," she concluded in green.

Another idea is to keep a notebook with two columns. Using a ruler as a guide, draw a line down the center of your notebook pages. Then write the facts in the left-hand column, leaving the right column free for your comments and questions to yourself.

A journal or daybook maintained over the years—like Thomas Jefferson's—provides a record of how your thinking has grown over time. In a few years, you may find it fascinating to go back through your notes to discover what interested you "way back when" and how you were sorting out the experiences of your life.

Observation Schedules. At some point, your learning will probably lead you to collecting information on a regular basis, and your notebook can be especially helpful here. Suppose you are interested in measuring the arrival of spring (something done by a group of young people in my area recently). You might use your notebook to record systematically—day by day or week by week—the disappearance of snow and ice (if you're in that part of the country), the blossoming of spring flowers, the emergence of bird and animal life. An observation schedule can also keep track of scientific experiments, with regular listings of information you collect.

Reading Notes. As a person interested in learning, you're probably also a reader of a wide range of material. Although you may want to clip and file some of what you read, for convenience it's often useful to write reading notes or summaries. Here again, don't just write down facts and quotes (although that will be a part of what you do). Always include your ideas about what's important and why. A good reading journal will be a kind of conversation with yourself (or even an imaginary conversation with the author of the book you are reading). It may also prove useful for you to index your reading notes, making a list of all the books and other materials that you've read and taken notes on.

Index Cards. I've emphasized note*books* in this section, and I personally like to keep my records in a three-ring binder where I can include clippings and other print materials. However, using index cards has some real advantages, including the fact that you can easily rearrange the cards as you organize your study. Index cards also have the advantage that they're small, so you can carry a packet of them around with you when you're heading off to the library on a **Quest.** You might also want to purchase a small ring binder specially designed to hold index cards. (That beats using rubber bands to hold them in a deck.) I've even seen packets of index cards in a spiral binding format, so you can tear them out as you need them.

Almost all the notetaking projects I've described in the previous pages can be done on index cards. You can maintain a daily or weekly learning log, journal, daybook, reading notes, school notes, or observation schedules all on your trusty pack of index cards. One warning and bit of advice: always put a date and "page" number on each card. That way if the cards become scrambled (which happens regularly) you can put them back into order again.

A Note on Documentation. "Documentation" simply means "keeping track of where things come from." In recording notes and information in notebooks or on index cards (or on the backs of envelopes or on scraps of paper if that's your style), it is important to develop the habit of *documenting*. If you read a newspaper article, jot down the name of the paper, the date, and the page number. If you're reading a book, make note of the publisher and date of publication as well as the name of the author and the title. If you copy down a quotation, make certain you write down who said it, on what occasion, and the name of the publication where you read it. If you are keeping an observation schedule, enter the date, the time, and the place of your observations. If you're writing a journal, put in the date, time, and even the place where you did your writing. Developing the habit of documentation will help you in school when you're preparing reports, but it will also be useful to you whenever you move beyond data collecting to reaching some conclusions about what you've gathered.

✳ ✳ ✳ QUESTING ✳ ✳ ✳

Organize your Learner's Notebook to include some of the note-taking forms described in this section. For example, you might want to add a section which contains a Page-a-Day, recording your observations and reactions to what you're seeing and learning. Use it as a journal or daybook. Put in a section for your reading notes. Experiment with keeping an observation schedule—say, of your own TV viewing habits or how you spend your days. When your first notebook is full, start another, then another. Eventually you may find that you want to create specific notebooks for specific tasks or projects—say, one for records of your collections, one for your daily journal, one for your reading. Or experiment with index cards as a variation of the Learner's Notebook. Get a packet of cards and start writing things on them. Then work out a filing system for these cards you are producing.

Drawing and Sketching

Don't forget that you can keep some interesting records using pencil and paper as drawing tools. "A picture is worth a thousand words," is the old maxim, and for some forms of record keeping that is absolutely true. Even if you don't feel you are particularly talented as an artist, you can often use stick figures or rough sketches to record everything from a scene in nature to preliminary plans for something you want to create or build. You can strengthen your skills as an artist by practicing them; the more you draw, the better you will become at it. If you are a reasonably accomplished drawer or painter already, you can use your skill as a way of recording what you've seen or experienced.

Using Media to Collect Data

"Media" are communication aids or tools that let you save information for later use. Marshall McLuhan, a Canadian scholar and media specialist, once described a *medium* as an extension of the human body. A tape recorder is thus a kind of extension of the ears, helping you listen better. A camera can be an extension of the eye. Most important, many media also serve as extensions of the human *brain* by letting you save more information than you can possibly remember. For instance, with a photograph you can preserve the details of a scene, where with memory alone (or with notes or sketches made with pencil and paper) you can only save part.

Of course, there can be problems with collecting information by use of media, because you can save so much information that you are overwhelmed by it. In this section, then, I'll suggest some ideas for using media *selectively,* not just to accumulate information, but to save the parts that will be useful to you later by reflecting your interests and point of view.

Audio Recorders

Home recorders have made a great deal of technological progress over the past forty or fifty years. When first invented, they were

✳ ✳ ✳ QUESTING ✳ ✳ ✳

See what you can learn through drawing. Your equipment can be simple: a lead pencil and a supply of paper. Or you can bring along a full line of artist's colored pencils, chalk, felt-tip markers, watercolors, acrylics and oils, and the appropriate surfaces for drawing or painting. Do some drawings and study them carefully. How does the act of drawing help you observe your world more closely than usual? What do you discover about your subject after you've finished your drawing? Try drawing:

· buildings around you, especially those where you spend a great deal of time

· rooms (or one wall of a room)

· people (Don't worry about trying to catch facial likenesses—concentrate on broad shapes and sizes, on impressions of people.)

· animals

· action scenes (Draw crowd scenes, traffic scenes, scenes on television and movies. Use stick figures if you can't draw bodies and faces well.)

· copies of pictures in magazines, or copies of photographs of friends and family members

· tracings of objects: leaves, pencils, combs

A good learning **Quest** would be for you to learn more about art and drawing. There are numerous "how to" books at your local library that can give you a few quick pointers on how to improve your art. As an offshoot, you might want to explore learning how to cartoon, which also requires you to see your subject clearly and to learn how to turn your observations into lines on a page.

bulky boxes using reels of tape (or, in some cases, wire) to capture sound. Microphones were also large and not very effective, so a home recording often made a person sound as if he or she were speaking from across a room.

Nowadays, recorders are small (and getting smaller) so they are easy to carry around with you and often have microphones built in. The old-fashioned reels of tape have been replaced by cassettes that you just pop into the machine. There is still a problem with the quality of sound of home recorders: usually the microphone must be within eighteen inches of a sound source to obtain high quality. That presents some problems if you want to tape a roomful of people talking or capture the chirp of a bird perched on top of yonder tree. Nevertheless, if you think about the possibilities, you'll see there are a number of ways you can use a tape recorder.

Sounds. Your ears are "turned on" twenty-four hours a day. Even when you're asleep, a noise like a smoke alarm or someone moving in the next room will wake you up. Much of the time, however, people listen quite selectively, tuning out the background noises or the sounds they don't particularly want to hear, to focus on what's important. Some people, for example, can concentrate or work in very noisy places, just shutting out the unwanted noise and centering their attention on the task close at hand. (Some people, however, *can't* shut out unwanted noise and need perfect quiet for work or study to proceed.)

Voices. Your cassette recorder can save you a lot of time writing things down. Where the old-fashioned idea of a newspaper reporter shows a person scribbling furiously in a notebook, the modern reporter is someone who sticks a microphone into somebody's face to get an interview. Both tape and paper and pencil have their uses, and the tape recorder will never eliminate the need for people to write down notes.

Here are some possibilities for using the recorder as a "data collector" of voices:

* * * QUESTING * * *

Go sound collecting with a recorder. First, just turn on the machine and save everything that comes your way. Record sounds for five minutes when you first get up in the morning. What are the sounds of your household? Then tape the first five minutes of sound when you go out of doors—what do you hear? Turn on the recorder in the school cafeteria and capture the hubbub. Turn it on in class (with the teacher's permission) to see what sorts of sounds you snare. Find a place "away from it all" and record the sounds of nature for five minutes. Then listen to all these tapes and sounds and see what they tell you about the world you live in. How much of what you hear every day goes "in one ear and out the other," not attracting your conscious attention?

also

Start a sound effects collection with your recorder. Tape such sounds as:

People talking	Basketball bouncing	Cat purring
Car starting	Car horns blaring	Door slamming
School band tuning	Showerer singing	Raindrops pitterpattering
Eaters eating (bleagh!)	Books falling	Dishwasher washing
Garbage disposaling	Vacuum cleaning	Footsteps falling
Door creaking	Dog barking	Whistler whistling

At your record store you may find commercial sound-effects recordings. You might see what sorts of sounds the professionals have collected. What is the use for all these sounds? 1) They help you understand your world better. 2) You can use them to create wonderful effects for school plays.

Prerecorded voices. You can tape the sound off TV and radio programs. (This is "legal" as long as you are using your recording for personal research or pleasure, not to sell.) You can record great moments in sports, parts of radio or TV documentaries (particularly shows that are giving information on a topic that interests you), sounds of important events (rocket blastoffs, news reports, celebrations of holidays). The university where I teach has a wonderful "voice library" with tapes of all kinds of famous people. Just by taping from radio and TV you can create your own voice library.

Interviews. Asking people questions about what they know is an especially useful way to get information. Whether you're collecting information on banjo playing, plastic, hats, or tennis, you can find experts who know and who can answer your questions.

Your own voice. A great many businesspeople use tape recorders as an easy way to keep track of their ideas. Along with maintaining a written journal, you might want to make a taped "daybook," talking to your tape recorder, say, five or ten minutes a day. After an interview, you can make a tape of your own reactions, reminding yourself of the important things your interviewer said. When you're in the middle of a science project, you can record some of your observations. Some writers even like to use the tape recorder to "give themselves dictation," that is, they tell a story or "write" a report into their cassette recorder, then listen to the tape and get the ideas down on paper.

Cameras

Cameras are a remarkable extension of the human eye. With the right kind of lens on your camera, you can see things smaller than the naked eye can detect, and you can see things much farther away than your eye would ordinarily permit. In our high tech society, cameras, like tape recorders, have become more and more convenient to use.

There are tiny pocket cameras that you can carry with you anyplace and use on the spur of the moment. Film has become "faster" so that you can take photographs in very dim light without the aid of a flash bulb. Instant cameras allow you to get pictures developed on the spot so you can see exactly what it is you have photographed. Experimental cameras already exist that will use a laser disk instead of film and will play back photos on a television screen.

"Still" cameras have always been popular with vacationers and with researchers, and you can easily think of dozens of things you can photograph as you go about learning more about your world. Consider your camera a research tool, and every time you're out learning, ask yourself the question, "How can I use photographs of this?"

Movie cameras, which allow you to capture action, have enjoyed popularity for many years, but they are rapidly being replaced by video cameras that let you record sound and images on electromagnetic tape. Video cameras keep getting smaller and smaller, and there are now some cameras on the market that can be carried in one hand, with no bulky batteries or tape deck to haul around. Unfortunately, video cameras and recording decks are still expensive. Not every learner can own a video outfit, but most *schools* do, and frequently if you let your teachers know you're interested in doing some learning on your own (or as part of a school project) you can arrange to use the equipment.

You can probably think of many things to do with a video camera right away, but spend some time watching television programs, especially news programs and documentaries. What sorts of film and video "clips" do you see on the six o'clock news? Can you do interviews similar to the ones on TV? (Of course you can.) Can you capture "footage" of sports events or storms? (Certainly.) Can you use a video camera to collect information as do researchers in nature shows? (Absolutely.)

In fact, a video camera is another remarkable extension of the human eye. It will let you speed up the action, slow it down, and even "freeze" it for a better look, so your mind can analyze more carefully. You can sometimes learn more from a video than you can from seeing an event or a phenomenon in nature "live."

The recorder part of your video outfit can probably be hooked up to record from the television. Thus you can save information as it comes across the TV. Study the weekly TV schedule to see what might be useful to record. Since many recorders are "programmable," you may be able to set a timer to record the shows you want, even if you're not home. There is some debate about the legality of making recordings from your TV and whether or not that violates copyright laws. In general, if you're recording to collect information (not, say, to "steal" a movie off TV to save the cost of buying or renting it), you are within fair and legal use.

Computers

In our age, computers are a revolutionary advancement in technology, changing the way we study, learn, save information, and even think. The word "document" has taken on new meaning, for it no longer necessarily means a sheet of paper with writing on it. A document may now be a collection of electronic bits of information stored on a computer disk, and businesspeople are developing the idea of a "paperless" office, where all messages and documents are stored electronically, with nary a scrap of paper in sight.

Perhaps the greatest part of this breakthrough is the development of the personal computer or "PC"—the Apples, Ataris, Radio Shacks, and Commodores that you see around school or possibly even have at home. When the first computers were invented almost fifty years ago, they were huge, occupying many rooms, and they processed information relatively slowly. The desktop PCs that you see today have as much power and more speed than many of the original giant machines. Like cassette recorders, computers keep getting smaller; there are already portable computers you can carry around like a typewriter. It's only a matter of time before pocket computers make today's PCs look like dinosaurs.

✳ ✳ ✳ QUESTING ✳ ✳ ✳

Go **Questing** with your camera, whatever kind you have. If you have a *still camera* spend some time looking at the world around you for interesting things to photograph. (A friend of mine does photographs of rust spots on metal, and, believe it or not, finds a great deal of beauty there.) If you haven't done a lot of photography, you might want to leave out the film and pretend you are shooting pictures until you are certain of how and what you want to shoot. Take pictures carefully, since film and developing are expensive, but keep practicing to sharpen your "photographer's eye."

If you're working with a *video camera,* you can often experiment very freely because you can erase your errors and keep on practicing until you get it right. Shoulder up the camera and head off into the world to see what you can capture on tape.

Also, as you become more interested in photography as a way of collecting information, be sure to look for books at your library (or at a photography or video shop) that will help you learn to do it more effectively. As you'll discover, there's much more to photography than simply pointing your camera and pressing a button. You might also want to check the library for collections of photographs in book form to study how professional photographers work.

Computers are terrific data collectors. A single "floppy disk" for a computer can hold 800K of information—that's 800,000 individual bits—or more. A "hard disk" for a PC may store twenty or fifty "megabytes"—that's two to five *million* pieces of information. To hold that much on index cards or on sheets of notepaper, you'd have to fill your study with boxes, bags, file cabinets, and trunks.

You may not need to store that much information, but computers will increasingly become the central way in which people store and retrieve all kinds of data. In addition, because computers can "talk" to one another through telephone linkups, different files of information can be transferred from one machine to another, all at the punch of a button. There are now international financial institutions that are actually nothing more than a computer, sitting unattended in a room, shifting funds back and forth from one account to another, keeping records of sales, and notifying various clients and customers of what's happening to their money.

There are several kinds of programs that may be helpful to you for conducting your research. (If you don't have access to a computer, you may want to skip this section.)

Desktop or Management Programs

These help you organize your life and learning. A desk manager will include places for you to store names, addresses, and telephone numbers. (If you have a telephone hookup, some of these programs will even dial the phone for you.) The program may include a calendar so you can write down and remember important dates and appointments (and some programs include an alarm clock that will remind you of them). You can use your desktop program to keep notes and memos to yourself ("Get to the library." "Call the newspaper to ask about pet care."), and you can keep various kinds of lists and records or a financial budget. These programs help you get *organized*. (For you non-computer users, remember, there's hardly anything in one of these programs that you can't do yourself with paper and pencil. "Getting organized" is a state of mind. Although a computer program can help you do that, it is no substitute for a desire to get things organized in the first place.)

Data File Programs

These programs save information and allow you to get it back easily. You can put in titles of books and get back an alphabetized list. You can type in names and addresses and get back a printout organized by names or by zip codes or by people who live in a particular city, state, or town. File programs work best for information that you collect regularly, in the same form, so if you are doing scientific observations, a data file program can be helpful to you. Data files can also be very helpful if you are a leader in any school clubs or extracurricular activities, because you can keep membership lists, make a record of dues paid, and even print out mailing labels for your newsletters or correspondence.

Graphics Packages

Many computer programs will let you prepare visual material, "drafting" your artwork on the screen, then printing out on paper. Some printers will even create color copies of your art. Depending on the kind of program you are using, you can do drawings, charts, graphs, even blueprints or designs. A good program in this category can be useful to you not only in reporting your research, but in planning what you want to do in the first place.

Word Processing Programs

For my money, a word processing program is the single most useful computer tool for the researcher. Essentially, a word processor turns your computer into a television typewriter that allows you to make changes on the screen. Word processors also have features like "search," which allows you to find key words in your document easily, and "block move," which lets you shift materials from one place to another. In school you may have worked with a word processing program like the Bank Street Writer or Scripsit, programs that are easy to learn to use.

   With a little imagination, you can also use your word processor for all sorts of **Questing** applications. You can use it to:

   · file information (Just like a data file program, except that you use the "search" function to find it.)

· keep notes (You can add in new material easily and even rearrange it in a more convenient pattern.)

· brainstorm for ideas and questions (Some people like to set aside a part of a computer disk for "bright ideas.")

· create a plan or outline for a report

Many word processing programs are now accompanied by spelling and grammar "checkers," which will read a report you've written and check to make certain you haven't made any major errors in correctness.

Telecommunications Programs

A computer can be hooked up to a telephone by a "modem," which, in turn, lets you communicate with other computers very easily. If you belong to a network like CompuServe or The Source, you can get information on everything from the stock market to transportation schedules. You can also use a telecommunications program to get involved with computer bulletin boards, where users send in questions or comments and get replies from other interested people.

The future of data collecting and sharing through computers sounds as if it's right out of science fiction. Even now computer specialists are experimenting with forms of storage using laser disks that will allow people to save three-dimensional images like holograms along with various other kinds of information. There are experimental programs that put holograms of whole cities on disk, keyed to a computer, so you can call up a picture of any street and see yourself walking down it. While it will be some time before you can do this sort of thing with your home computer, we can now imagine systems that combine video, graphics, sound, and numbers, so a person could record all the kinds of information I have described in this chapter in a computer. It's quite possible to imagine scientific record keeping, where pictures or videos of, say, a flower growing, are saved along with various kinds of measurements, all with the voice of the scientist commenting about what's happening. In fact, computer technologists

---

✳ ✳ ✳ COMPUTERQUEST ✳ ✳ ✳

Lots of schools now have courses in "computer literacy," in which students have a chance to become familiar with computers and how they work. If you've had such a course you may even have learned how to do a little programming of a computer using a language like Basic or Logo. Those courses will help you get started using a computer. However, the most important thing for the learner to do is think of ways to make the computer serve his or her particular needs. There are lots of people who just don't bother to think of what the computer can do to help them. So I encourage you to explore and experiment to see what interesting things you can do with it. Try different ways of storing data on your computer. Think about ways in which you can take advantage of telephone networks. Try doing some of your homework or schoolwork using art or graphics packages to liven things up. Every time you start a **Quest,** ask yourself, "How can I take advantage of all the wonderful features of my computer?" Pretty soon you'll find that you "think creatively" about computers, coming up with uses that aren't really described in the program manuals, but which make your life as a learner much easier.

---

are already at work trying to develop programs that will recognize speech sounds and convert them into letters and words; when that happens, you'll be able to "talk" your data into the computer and it will take dictation from you.

4 Look It Up— Print and Media Sources

Never preface an inquiry to a librarian with, "I know this is a stupid question, but. . . ."

There are no stupid questions.

WILLIAM KATZ, *Your Library*, p. 8

In his book *Finding Facts,* William Rivers tells the story of a newspaper editor who boasted that one of his reporters had spent more than $250 making phone calls all over the country to get some important information for a story. Then the editor discovered that the very same information was available to the reporter free of charge in a public library just a few hundred yards down the street. (The story doesn't tell what happened to the reporter once his editor made his discovery.)

Much of this chapter is about *libraries*, which are interesting places, packed full of information, most of it accessible to you at no cost. More important, however, is that this chapter is dedicated to the idea that you can find answers to a great many of your questions right in your own neighborhood, by looking things up. I'll discuss some of the newer methods of information storage, including computers, films, and tape, but the principal resources I will describe are in dependable print: books, magazines, pamphlets, and newspapers.

Writing is a remarkable method human beings have invented for storing information. In a book or manuscript or even on a single page you can store all sorts of ideas that might be lost if left solely to the brain. Prior to the development of the printing press, books and manuscripts had to be copied by hand. Even though that was tedious, it allowed people to preserve their knowledge so it could be shared, passed along to people in the next generation. When printing was developed in the sixteenth century, the gateway was open to even more use of print and books, putting the accumulated knowledge of the world at the disposal of every person. Even the new media forms like films, filmstrips, and cassette recordings draw heavily on writing as part of the storage and retrieval processes.

Almost as soon as writing evolved, people created places where manuscripts could be stored: libraries. The word *library* comes from the Latin *liber,* meaning book, but the history of libraries can be traced back to ancient Mesopotamia, about 3000 years ago, long before the existence of books as we know them, when bulky clay tablets covered with writing were stored in palaces and temples. At first, libraries were largely the property of the powerful or wealthy; hand copied documents were just too expensive for the common person to own. Many libraries were the property of churches, which used them as places to store religious documents. The Egyptian kings had libraries; the Greeks developed libraries for scholarly use; and the Romans followed suit. Today, whether you live in a small or large town, the odds are there are school and public libraries available to you that contain more books than you could possibly read in a lifetime.

Unfortunately, some learners—young and old—are a bit turned off or scared off by libraries. Even a small library can be an imposing place, and you can feel silly or stupid or lost—"How can I find what I want amongst all this *stuff?*" As you approach a library, you should remember what William Katz said in the epigraph that begins this chapter: "There are no stupid questions." Most librarians are eager to help learners, and if you go to them with questions, you'll get good help and answers.

You've probably had guided tours of the library in school (or you will have them more than once before you've finished your studies), so I'm not going to give very specific details on how to use a library. Even better than tours, I think, is learning "in the flesh," poking around in your own school or public library, seeing how it works, getting help when you need assistance. However, I do want to tell you a little about how libraries work and the kinds of things you can discover from and through them. Then, lest I give the impression that libraries are the only places where you can look things up, I'll describe some other sources of information that are available in your school or community.

Starting with Questions

In Chapter 2 I discussed question asking. If you did some of the suggested **Quests,** you developed lists of topics that interest you and some "balloons" of questions about some of those topics.

A **Quest** at a library begins with good **quest**ions. William Rivers suggests that there are three basic kinds you can ask:

Directional—where are things located in the library: Where are the magazines? the encyclopedias? the bathrooms?

Ready Reference—basic facts that can be looked up in materials in the library: What's the capital of the Ukraine? Who won the 1942 American League batting championship? How many nuclear power plants are there in the world?

Research Questions—topics that deal with ideas and concepts rather than specific answers: What kinds of career opportunities are there in the theater? How good or bad are junk foods for your body?

In *The Young Learner's Handbook* we're mostly interested in the third kind of question, the research question, although a number of questions of the second kind, ready reference, are a part of any **Quest.** The directional questions are the kinds you can answer best at your local library.

To focus your learning and your learning about the library, it's best to go there with a specific set of questions like the ones you asked in Chapter 2, preferably written down. It's *not* such a great idea to walk up to the librarian and simply ask, "What have you got on nuclear power?" More focused questions might be: "What kind of information do you have on safety regulations for nuclear power plants?" Or even better, "Can you get me started finding out some information on safety in nuclear power plants?"

Don't expect the librarian to do your research for you; that's not his or her job. However, you can expect that if you go in with focused questions, you'll find the librarian helpful in giving you the *directional* advice you need: "Here's our card catalog. Why don't you try looking up books under the heading of nuclear power? After you've finished with that, let me show you how to use the *Reader's Guide to Periodical Literature.*"

Encyclopedias

One of the first things you'll probably want to know is where the encyclopedias are stored. Like writing and libraries, encyclopedias have been around for a long time. In fact, many of the people who were most interested in libraries—men like the Greek philosopher, Aristotle, and the Roman scholar, Varro—also considered writing books that would compile large amounts of information in one place. That's essentially what an encyclopedia is: a collection of information in book form. (The word comes from the Greek *enkyklios* [en-keek-lee-ohs], meaning "general," and *paideia* [pie-dee-ah], meaning "education.")

There are all sorts of encyclopedias: encyclopedias of sports, cooking, health, medicine, politics, and government. When most of us speak of "the encyclopedia," however, we mean a multiple-volume collection of general information, usually found in the reference section of the library.

Encyclopedias are good news and bad news for the learner. The good news is that within an encyclopedia you will find an enormous amount of data on practically every topic ever thought of by humankind. Encyclopedias are usually arranged alphabetically: *B* for behavior, *N* for nuclear power, *U* for the Ukraine. The articles are usually fairly short (at least compared to a book), and they are written by experts in the field to insure accuracy and reliability. Encyclopedias are revised and updated every few years, and some of them include yearbooks or annual supplements to keep the information up to date.

The best known and most frequently used encyclopedias are the *Britannica* (which is the most complete and, unfortunately, the most difficult to read), the *Americana, Collier's,* and the *World Book.* You can check to see which your library has, and after using different ones, you can decide which works best for you.

The bad news about encyclopedias is that they are so easy to use that often learners never go beyond them. Students are often required to write school reports, and they learn how to use encyclopedias quickly (and *wrongly*), looking up the topic in the book and copying down the facts. Unfortunately, the information is often not very detailed, and, more important, the learners just don't *learn* very much by lifting material from an encyclopedia and just copying it in a report.

I suggest that when you're starting a **Quest** it is a good idea to check one or more encyclopedias to get an overview of your subject—the basic ideas. Don't copy the information you find there (although you might want to make a few notes). Instead, with your basic knowledge from the encyclopedia, head off to the rest of the library to find the richly detailed information that rests on the shelves. (Some encyclopedias will list the titles of books that go into topics in much more detail, so your encyclopedia reading can help you find specific books that you'll want to seek out elsewhere in the library.)

The Card Catalog

The key to getting at the rest of the materials in the library is the card catalog, which you've certainly seen in your school or public library. Usually the catalog consists of trays of index cards, each card listing an item the library has in its collection. The cards are arranged in alphabetical order, but the catalog is more than an A–Z listing of books. It represents a solution to a rather complicated question, "How do you arrange or classify what people know?"

The problem of classification has worried and intrigued scholars and thinkers for a long time. The Greek philosopher Aristotle was a famous classifier of knowledge about the natural world, inventing a system for separating living creatures into subcategories, a scheme that was widely used until just two hundred years ago. Fifteen centuries after Aristotle, the British philosopher and writer, Sir Francis Bacon (also an encyclopedist), puzzled over the same question: "How do we arrange what we know?" Today, with the explosion of knowledge and research, there are people at work trying to figure out classification systems, especially systems that can be computerized.

There are many different ways in which a person can classify or divide knowledge, and most of those influence how we arrange books on library shelves. Thus, Thomas Jefferson, that voracious reader of all kinds of books, worked carefully on a system for the library shelves in his home in Monticello, Virginia. If you visit Monticello, you will see many of his books on the shelves, still in the order in which he placed them.

The books on the shelves of your school or public library are *not* in simple alphabetical order like the card catalog or an encyclopedia. You *don't* find all the books beginning with *A* near the front door and the *Z* books near the rear exit. Instead, books (and other materials) are grouped by similar classifications. If you're interested in bugs, for example, you'll find the bug books together, close to books about other kinds of living creatures. If you want to learn more about nuclear energy you'll find those titles grouped together, close to other books about science.

The system most commonly used to group books was developed by a librarian, Melvil Dewey, in 1876. Dewey divided knowledge into nine broad classifications and assigned each one a series of numbers in the hundreds:

000–099   *General works,* "among them encyclopedias, and general periodicals—which contain so many different kinds of information that they do not fit into any other class"

100–199   *Philosophy,* "conduct of life"

200–299   *Religion,* "nature and meaning of life"

300–399   *Social sciences,* "man's relations with his fellows"

400–499   *Language,* "human communication"

500–599   *Pure Science,* "observation of man's environment"

600–699   *Technology,* "manipulation of man's environment"

700–799   *The Arts,* "enrichment of life"

800–899   *Literature,* "thoughts about life"

900–999   *History,* "examination of the past"

(Rivers, p. 78)

Dewey's system is especially interesting because it is more than just a way of grouping books; it reveals his view of how people function in the world. Thus each one of his categories is concerned with how learning helps people: to understand themselves (through philosophy and religion, for example), to discover their relationships with other people (social science and language), to explore the world in which they live (science), to examine their control over the world (technology), to develop their sense of beauty (art), and to deepen their understanding of how people have behaved in the world (literature and history).

Dewey went farther and broke his system into smaller units, so that within the arts, for example, you will find that books on painting are in the 760s and books on music are in the 780s. Every book in the library has to fit in someplace, with those that don't slide into any category easily falling into the "general" books, numbered 000–099. The "decimal" in the Dewey *Decimal* System refers to even more subdivisions which are indicated by a decimal point and one or several numbers. A book called *Our Bodies, Our Selves* is logged into the library at 301.41 among the books on social science. One titled *Records in Review* carries the longer number of 789.913 in the arts/music category.

One problem with the Dewey system is that as knowledge grows and the shelves become crowded, more and more decimals have to be introduced to classify a book.

A different library system, developed by the Library of Congress in 1897, attempts to solve that problem. It is most popular with very large libraries, such as those in colleges or universities. The "L.C." system is arranged this way, using letters of the alphabet:

A	General Works	M	Music
B	Philosophy—Religion	N	Fine Arts
C	History	P	Language and Literature
D	Topography (maps)	Q	Science
E–F	America	R	Medicine
G	Geography—Anthropology	S	Agriculture
H	Social Sciences	T	Technology
J	Political Sciences	U	Military Science
K	Law	V	Naval Science
L	Education	Z	Bibliography

Although the L.C. system is more easily expandable than the Dewey system, there are still gaps and problems. For example, in 1897 Military Science and Naval Science were more important than they are today, yet they still take up two letters of the L.C. alphabet. If you were a modern day classifier, you might want to reduce those two categories in favor of developing a new one, say, "Rocketry Science." A problem with any system is that once the library has started using it, the librarian finds it difficult, if not impossible, to change over. (My university library was on the Dewey system once upon a time, then changed over to L.C. I still find old books that have not been reclassified, and before I can check them out, a person at the front desk has to change over the number.)

For your purposes, it doesn't matter a great deal which system— Dewey or L.C.—is in use. What you need to know is that the "call number"—printed on the spine of the book and listed in the library catalog—is simply a way of assigning each book in the library a number that is unique, so you can find the book easily and so the librarian can return it to its proper spot on the shelves when you're through. Once you've learned the Dewey or Library of Congress number, you can find the book you want.

A card catalog is generally divided into three sections, listing books by author, title, or subject. I find the subject catalog most helpful in my own research, since I can go directly to the topic I want to study and see what sorts of books the library has. I also enjoy "perusing" the subject catalog, just flipping through the cards to see what sorts of topics are listed there. Often I find subjects and areas of knowledge that I didn't even know I was interested in. The results of one of my forays through the subject catalog are shown in Figure 4-1, an alphabetical listing of topics from A to Z that I would like to know more about. Would any of those subjects interest you?

The High Tech Library

Earlier I said that *usually* the library catalog is a series of trays containing index cards. However, many libraries are now using computers, either as an alternative to the card catalog or as a side-by-

---

FIGURE 4-1:   Topics for Investigation from the Subject Catalog

Aberdeen-Angus cattle	Gordon, Flash	Table manners
Addiction	Holograms	United Nations
Arctic expeditions	Knighthood	Urban renewal
Baton twirling	Mars	Vandalism
Berlin Wall	Mice	Walking
Cacti	Needles	Water power
Child abuse	Noodles	Weather
Cyclones	Origami	X-rays
Demonology	Pain	Xerography
Earth, origins of	Paint	Yarn
Electronic data	Personality tests	Yucatan
processing	Quartets, barbershop	Zebras
Ferrets	Quartets, string	Zero
Food synthesis	Savings	Zoos
Genetic cloning	Schools	

---

side system. Increasingly, you will begin your search for material at a computer terminal, punching in subject, author, or title and getting a video display or printout of available materials. Instead of cards tucked into pockets in the backs of books, many libraries are using "bar codes" like the zebra-stripe price marks on supermarket items. When you check out a book, a laser scanner "reads" the bar code and stores the information in the same library computer. When you look up a book using the computer terminal, you can be told whether that book is checked out at the moment. Some libraries have computerized indexes to magazines as well. Eventually libraries will come to have all their information files linked together and linked to the files of other libraries. When that day comes, working at a computer terminal (perhaps even in your own home) you can unearth incredible amounts of information about your subject.

---

* * * QUESTING * * *

Explore the card catalog at your school or public library. Spend some time studying the cards to see all the information that is given on them. (Often your librarian will have prepared a sheet explaining how to "read" the cards.) If you have a favorite author, look up his or her name in the author catalog to see how many books your library has. Then cross check some of that author's titles to see how they are listed in the title catalog. Cruise through the subject catalog looking for topics from A to Z that interest you. When you discover a topic, copy down the call numbers of several books and locate them in the library. Don't be bashful about asking for help!

or

Begin **Questing** on one of the topics you've entered into your Young Learner's Notebook: Study the questions that you've written for yourself and begin searching for books that will hold the answers you want.

Microfilm is a technology that is not quite so new, having been around for most of this century. It has revolutionized some library collections. Microfilms (sometimes in versions called microform or microfiche) are simply photographs of text pages which can be read on a machine that projects them to their original size. Microfilm allows the library to turn fat books into small rolls of film or sheets of negatives about the size of an index card. Some libraries have replaced the traditional card catalogue with a microfilm file. Many libraries put their daily newspapers on microfilm to save space. Older books that do not circulate are sometimes filmed rather than thrown away, and frequently you can find microfilmed copies of books that are valuable or scarce. Thus even though your school or local library may be tiny in physical size, it could have a huge number of publications on file. With some microfilm machines you can also obtain a photocopy of what's on the screen, giving you "hard copy" to take away with you.

Some experts predict that microfilm use will decrease in the future, because texts can be stored even more easily on computer disks. In the future, then, you may call up an electronically "scanned" image of your daily paper on a computer screen and read that (or you might request a printout, a "facsimile" or look-alike of the page, complete with photographs).

There's more high tech in the library's future:

Some libraries are beginning to collect holograms, three-dimensional photographs made with laser light to be viewed under a special light projector.

Telephone "modems" are now linked to library systems, allowing a user to find out information by typing in requests in the comfort of his/her home.

Tapes, films, and videos will increasingly be stored on laser disks and indexed by computer. In fact, there are experimental projects already under way that link library resources together in a "multimedia" format.

Imagine the possibilities: As you read a play, you can call up film clips of important scenes and watch how various actors and actresses have presented that scene over the years. As you research a news event, you can call up copies of the newspapers of the day and then tune into a tape of the six o'clock news from that very day. If you're interested in visiting a city far away, you may be able to call up written information about it, obtain maps, scan the phone directory, and even see holographic, "3-D" pictures of the main street.

You can see, then, that even as knowledge grows more and more complex, high tech library devices will make information more and more easily available to you.

---

* * * QUESTING * * *

Learn about the high tech equipment in your library. (Hint: Most of this equipment has an electrical plug; just look for plugs in the wall and see what's on the other end.) If your library is not yet computerized, ask the librarian about any plans. Find out what other electronic devices and gizmos are available to make your life as a young learner easier and more productive.

What Else Does the Library Hold?

The modern library is much more than a collection of books. In fact, many school libraries are called media centers because they hold many nonprint information sources such as microfilms, films, tapes, and records. However, libraries go even farther by offering special services, collections, and information aids. In addition to books, newspapers, and magazines, a library may include:

· a reference service (with a librarian to help you find specific answers to your "ready reference" questions and to assist you in locating books)

· recordings and cassette tapes (of literature, music, old-time radio, sound effects, famous events in history, "how-to" instructions)

· audio-visual equipment that can be borrowed (record player, cassette player, microfilm reader, 8-millimeter film projector, filmstrip projector, 16-millimeter film projector, videocassette player)

· videocassette library (with a number of films and self-improvement tapes)

· film library (with 16-millimeter movies that can be ordered in advance for use at everything from a school demonstration to a birthday party)

· filmstrip collection

· telephone directories (for most major cities as well as towns and cities around the state)

· consumer information (with books, magazines, and buying guides)

· medical reference materials (books, pamphlets, lists of places to call for help)

· aids for the hearing and visually impaired (large-print books for people with poor eyesight, books in braille for the totally blind, recorded books)

· local history collections (with newspapers, photographs, clippings, and recorded interviews)

· community notebooks (listings of classes and coming events, services for the elderly and handicapped, activities for children, summer camps and programs, storytelling festivals, puppet shows, puzzle collections)

· art rental collection

· program listings (lectures, concerts, discussions on all manner of topics)

· catalogs (for colleges and universities, for shopping at home)

Not every school or public library will have the same features, but many have these, plus other features such as computers and word processors, copy centers, leaflets on how-to-do-it projects, and even catalogs for college and university classes.

Reference Books

In a Dewey Decimal library, you'll find hundreds of fascinating books filed in the 000–009 section, general reference. (In a Library of Congress classification, they're under the letter *A*.) Everybody knows about encyclopedias and dictionaries, which are the most common books found in the reference collection. Here are some other reference books that illustrate the range of resources available to you:

✳ ✳ ✳ QUESTING ✳ ✳ ✳

What does *your* library have besides books? You will probably find an information leaflet describing resources at the main desk. It will tell you the collections in the library and where they will be found. If the library is not physically large, you might prefer to spend some time just wandering around getting acquainted with the resources and their locations. You'll probably find the record collection easily enough; then locate where the magazines and newspapers are stored. If you've begun a **Quest** topic, see what sorts of nonbook materials your library has to help you learn more about it.

John Bartlett, *Bartlett's Familiar Quotations.* Boston: Little, Brown, revised regularly. (This famous reference book has been around in various editions for more than 125 years. It contains quotable quotes from many well-known people and indexes them by various topics. It's an easy way to locate the source of a familiar quote or to find a useful one for use in a report.)

Marjorie Adolf Cohen, *Whole World Handbook.* New York: E.P. Dutton, 1981. (This book is a guide to work and study abroad. If you've ever thought about traveling to another country, before you graduate from high school or after, this book will help you find out places to go and how to get there.)

Pierre Grimal, *Larousse World Mythology.* New York: G.P. Putnam's, revised regularly. (Everything you ever wanted to know about myths and legends from around the world: India, the Germanic countries, Russia, the Orient, Eskimo, American Indian, South America. . . .)

Maurice Horn, *World Encyclopedia of Comics.* New York: Chelsea House, 1976. (Information on cartoons, comics, and comic artists.)

Index to Handicrafts, Model Making, and Workshop Projects. Westwood, Massachusetts: F. W. Faxon, revised and updated regularly. (This publication indexes thousands of magazines with hobby and craft information and tells you about developments in crafts from airplane models to yarn toys.)

Joseph Kane, *Famous First Facts.* New York: H. W. Wilson, 1961. (A book for the trivia nut, with records on "firsts," divided by topic, year, and even days of the year.)

Literary Market Place. New York: R. R. Bowker, issued annually. (The "bible" of the book writing and book publishing industries, with information on where to send materials to get published, contests for writers, and miscellaneous information useful to the young or experienced writer.)

Leonard Martin, *TV Movies.* New York: New American Library, updated frequently. (Indexes 16,000 movies you're likely to see on cable, pay, or regular TV channels.)

Clifford Moore, *The Book of Wild Pets.* Boston: Charles Branford, 1954. (How to care for such beasts as frogs, toads, salamanders, snakes, turtles, lizards, alligators, spiders, crayfish, owls, ducks, pigeons, geese, rabbits, racoons, snakes, or other beasts of the field or pond you might capture or find injured and take home.)

The Oxford English Dictionary. London: Oxford University Press, revised regularly. (You've not seen a dictionary until you've looked at this one, which attempts to include *every* word in the English language, along with its origins in history and its current use. The *OED* is not the sort of dictionary you'd use in school for reports—it contains sixteen volumes plus several supplements—but it's a wonderful place to search and browse for fascinating information about the language we use every day of our lives.)

Jerome Rosow, *Made in America.* New York: Facts on File,

1984. (12,000 products that are made in the United States, from clothing to cars to shoes to chemicals.)

Ann Sequoia, *The Complete Catalogue of Mail Order Kits.* New York: Rawson, Wade, 1981. (If you like to build things, check this sourcebook for kits to make anything from a fishing pole to a log house.)

Myron Smith, *Cloak-and-Dagger Bibliography.* Metuchen, New Jersey: Scarecrow Press, 1976. (Like spy stories? This book indexes major American mystery books of this century.)

Mort Weisinger, *1001 Valuable Things You Can Get Free.* New York: Bantam, updated frequently. (Like free things? Don't mind writing letters? This is the reference book for you.)

∗ ∗ ∗ QUESTING ∗ ∗ ∗

Find the reference section in your library and browse for books that interest you. For every one I've listed here you'll find a dozen more curious, odd, comprehensive, and amazing books to help "reference" you to your world.

Learning From Other Sources

Library resources go on and on (as I'm sure you can tell). But not all useful information is found in the library, and there are plenty of other places where you can go in your community to find information in print and nonprint forms. Here are some ideas about places to visit:

Bookstores

Unlike a library, a bookstore doesn't require you to use a card catalog; the books are divided by categories like history, science, self-help, and fiction. You simply find the section you want (ask for help from a clerk if you are uncertain) and look at the books to see if one fits your interests. More and more bookstores are also carrying cassette tapes of recorded literature and how-to information.

Used bookstores and paperback exchanges are excellent places to visit, especially if you're short on money. Although books wear out, there's no reason to avoid buying a "previously owned text," which will read just as well as a new one.

A newer kind of "bookstore" in the United States is the *video store*, which stocks videotapes for home rental. There are stores that specialize in videos, and even the neighborhood convenience or snack store may have a few tapes for rent. While many of these tapes are simply for home entertainment, you will also find videos that will be

---

✳ ✳ ✳ COMPUTERQUEST ✳ ✳ ✳

An important new electronic "library" for the computer user is the commercial reference source. You pay a fee to join and then are charged every time you use the system, which is accessed through your computer and a telephone modem. When you first come "on line" with one of these services, you are given a computer menu with a number of choices to make. Depending on your interests, you can tap into national news, electronic banking, shopping catalogs, financial information, travel schedules, mini-encyclopedias, other computer programs, bulletin boards, and educational and other games. Your local computer dealer will have a sample program to show you how this sort of electronic resource works, or the sponsors (look for their ads in computer magazines) will often give you a free or inexpensive trial look at the system. If you (or your school or somebody you know) has a computer modem, you might want to look into this kind of futuristic information service.

useful to you in your learning and research. From time to time stop by a well-stocked video center and look through its catalog.

Newspapers

I'm a kind of "newspaper addict" and love to read the paper first thing in the morning. I often find articles on topics of interest to me and regularly clip out articles to save for future use. It's interesting how often you'll find articles that bear directly on a topic you are studying. The very day that I wrote this page, for example, I came across a newspaper article about a library that is converting to computerized "card" catalogs, and that was useful to me in writing this chapter.

Magazines

In the past twenty years, magazine publishers have learned how to "target" publications for particular groups of people or "populations." This allows them to create a magazine for just about any special interest group. If you own a Commodore computer, there's a magazine for you. (You'll also find specialized magazines for your Apple or IBM.) If you train dogs, you can learn about people who share that interest in several magazines. Some good magazines that might be of interest to you are shown in Figure 4-2. Which of them have you seen?

You can buy magazines at your local bookstore (or subscribe to them by mail), but don't forget that your local library subscribes to a great many, very likely some of the ones that would be helpful to you. Ask for the *serials list* to learn which magazines the library receives (or look in the reading room, where most of the current issues will be displayed).

An excellent reference book for magazines is the *Reader's Guide to Periodical Literature*, available at your library. Within the *Reader's Guide* you'll find indexes to a great many magazines on a vast array of topics. Magazines often give you more up-to-date information than books, which makes them especially useful if you want to stay at the forefront of knowledge in your special interest areas.

FIGURE 4-2:   Some Magazines for Learning

American Art and Antiques
American Craft
American Film
American Forests
American Heritage
American Photographer
Analog: Science Fact/Fiction
Animal Welfare
Armchair Detective
Audubon
Backpacker
Baseball Digest
Bicycling
Boys' Life
Car and Driver
Cat Fancy
Changing Times
Chess Life and Review
Compute!
Conservationist
Cricket
Dance
Dog Fancy
Field & Stream
Flying
Football Digest
Guitar Player
High Fidelity
Hobbies
Home Mechanics
Hot Rod
Life
Mad

Model Airplane News
Model Railroader
Modern Photography
National Geographic
Natural History
Newsweek
Outdoor Life
Popular Mechanics
Popular Photography
Popular Science
Quilter's Magazine
Railroad Model Craftsman
Ranger Rick
Reader's Digest
Rockhound News
Runner's World
Saturday Evening Post
Science
Science Digest
Seventeen
Skiing
Sky and Telescope
Sport
Sports Illustrated
Teen
Time
U.S. News and World Report
Woodshedder
Workbench
Writer
Writer's Digest
Yoga Journal

Books for Young Adults

You're holding one in your hands. Books for young adults are those written especially for people in your age bracket. Unfortunately, some of these YA books are "written down," underestimating your skills as a person and reader by going on in a sort of written baby talk. The best YA books, however, are lively, interesting, challenging, and well written. You'll find them filed separately at most bookstores and probably in your library.

There are many different kinds of YA books—browse through the collection at the library to see what's there. Those I think you'll find most helpful as a young learner are:

Nonfiction books. These are "true"—not fiction—books, exploring a wide range of topics. I think they're generally a lot more interesting than school textbooks, so if you're bored with geography, history, science, or math or if you find the text uninteresting, consider going to the library to look for nonfiction books on those topics.

Fiction. Fiction is a made-up tale—a novel, a short story—but good fiction is anything but "false" or "a lie." Fiction should be true to life. Even science fiction and fantasy, which deal with imaginary worlds, describe recognizable people (even when they're elves or aliens) so that a human reader can learn from them. A novel or short story can help you learn about yourself and about the world we live in. Don't make the mistake of quoting from a fictional book as if it were true, but do consider that fiction is sometimes as true or truer to life than some nonfiction.

Biography. The stories of people's lives have always fascinated me, and you'll find that the YA collection at your school or college library is packed with biographies of exciting people, including some who are not necessarily famous but who have led productive lives. You can learn factual information from a biography, but more important, you can get a strong sense of how people think, feel, and act. You can, to use a cliché, learn "lessons of life" from studying biography.

✳ ✳ ✳ QUESTING ✳ ✳ ✳

Earlier in the chapter I noted that people have long been interested in arranging books and other materials so they can find what they want easily. Library plans are also interesting reflections on the human mind and what it values. Now, your own personal library might not be very large, but you might still find it challenging to think about arranging the "stuff" in your learning center. You could sort through your books, records, magazines, newspaper clippings, and even collections like stamps, insects, or soft drink cans. Look for ways to cluster or group your "holdings." You may find that you want to create subcategories within collections; that is, you'd group your clippings differently than you would your collection of spy novels. Some people even catalog their home libraries, filling out an index card (or making an entry in a notebook or a computer) with each item they have, along with its location.

5 Learning from People

I once chatted with a man who worked as a freelance writer selling articles to a number of magazines and newspapers. Since freelancers must be very efficient writers—you have to sell many articles to make a living—I asked him to share some of his techniques: how did he go about getting the information he needed to develop a story?

"Never start at the library," was his advice. That surprised me, for I usually go to the library first when I want to learn something new, and I have generally advised my students to do the same.

"Find out who knows and talk to them," the writer continued. "There's always somebody around who knows the answers to the questions that I ask, and it's just quicker to talk than to read."

He went on to say that he is not opposed to books and libraries, and he uses them regularly in his research.

"I wore out my library card," he explained. "It was one of those computerized plastic kinds, and I used it so much I wore the magnetic strip right off the back."

Nevertheless, his experience as a writer had demonstrated the value of using people as a resource for learning.

81

I still do much of my **Questing** in the library, but I have since taken the journalist's advice. Before I spend a great deal of time thumbing through the card catalog, I make certain that I've made an effort to "find out who knows and talk to them."

Human beings are remarkable storehouses of information.

The owner's manual for my computer boasts that my machine has 512 kilobytes of memory, 512,000 separate bits of information that it can retrieve almost instantly. That seems very impressive until I recall that the human brain, much smaller than the computer, holds tens of millions of individual cells, each one storing bits of information. Further, the mind is quicker than even the fastest computer: a half dozen ideas will sometimes flash through my head while I sit at the console waiting for my computer to find something in its memory.

Here's another comparison with the human brain: my university library contains two and a half million books and magazines (and who knows how many words and numbers within those publications?). I can go to the library and look up all sorts of amazing bits of information. But my brain has also stored away an enormous amount of data. I'm astonished that it calls up images and memories from my childhood (something no library book can do) or can tell me in an instant who won the Kentucky Derby in 1942 or 1969, all without the trouble of a trip across campus. Although the sum total of information stored in the library is greater than that in my brain, much of that material is not something I need anyway.

"Static" information sources like books, libraries, films, cassettes, and computers are extraordinarily helpful to a learner. They are also *comprehensive* (*my* brain cannot tell me who won the Kentucky Derby in 1934 or 1952 or 1986, though I can look it up in the library). Books compile information; memories select and categorize it. What books and computer memory banks lack in speed they often make up in detail. Also, the speed and selectivity of the human brain can be a disadvantage, for minds are often very opinionated and are even known to give out quick but *wrong* information. A disk jockey on one of our local stations moans that every time he's about to ask a woman for a date, his brain, without warning, reminds him of all the times in his past he was turned down for a date, thus undercutting his confidence. He says he wishes he could erase those past bad memories as easily as you can erase a computer disk.

When you learn from people, you are opening up enormous brainpower, but a source you have to treat with great caution. You can't just assume that anything a person tells you is true, honest, or accurate. (Of course, you shouldn't assume that everything you read in print is true, honest, or accurate, either, since writing comes from people, not machines.) You need to judge and appraise: Is this person an expert? Is he/she likely to give me reliable information? Can I doublecheck these facts?

The "moral" of this chapter, then (I'll give it to you now rather than at the end), is "Find out who knows, and talk to them, *but* keep on relying on a variety of information sources."

People Sources: Some Ways to Learn

Observing people is an especially good way to learn. You've probably seen young children imitating their older brothers and sisters and their parents: dressing like them, acting like them, talking like them. It's cute when younger children do that. Their imitation is not simply a form of flattery; it's evidence of an observing mind at work learning. As a baby in the crib you began observing others, even before your eyes could clearly focus and make full sense of the world around you. There's no doubt that you continue to learn from observing people today. Who is wearing the current fashions at your school and what are those fashions? How does the best athlete in your school walk (can you imitate him or her)? What mannerisms of gesture or speech does your best friend have? Can you talk like any of the teachers? Can you imitate the dialect of someone who comes from another part of the country or the world? All that knowledge is evidence of your skill at observing people. Without your even being aware of it, your mind has studied those people and drawn some conclusions about what they wear, how they act, how they stand or wave their arms, how they talk.

---

* * * QUESTING * * *

Observing is a skill you can cultivate. In fact, although observing often takes place unconsciously, there's some reason to believe that if you do not practice it, you tend to lose the skill, to lose your freshness of observation. If you've ever read any of Arthur Conan Doyle's Sherlock Holmes stories, you know that the famous detective had cultivated his powers of observation to a high degree. From studying how a person walked or from analyzing a bit of suntan on the back of the hands, Holmes could tell remarkable things about who people were and where they had come from. Practice your powers of observation. Select people at school, at home, on the street, and study them for a period of time. After they have left your ken, write down your observations in your Learner's Notebook. At first just concentrate on recalling physical details: How tall is the person? Is she dark or light? What kinds of clothing was he wearing? Then as you become more and more adept and practiced as an observer, make generalizations about the person. Does he or she seem friendly? aloof? athletic? nonathletic? smart? not-so-smart? You won't always be able to check out those generalizations, but it should nevertheless prove interesting for you to speculate.

You can also use your powers of observation to learn new skills. You can watch a person row, swim, jump, play badminton, put together a model, sew, or change a tire and pretty much learn how it's done. Not everything in the world can be learned this way, but it's a useful beginning: watch how others do it; then go out and do likewise.

***

* * * QUESTING * * *

Apply your observational powers to a skill or activity you'd like to master: a sport, hobby, or craft. Study people who know how to do it well. Write down your observations. Watch people who do it badly—the losers, to put it bluntly. What differences do you see between those who do it well and those who don't? After you have learned all you think you can learn from observation, try to do the task yourself. What have you learned through observation?

(*Footnote:* Psychologists have discovered that some skills are much more complicated than they seem. Riding a bicycle doesn't *look* that difficult: you just get on and pedal. But as you probably know, bicycling is a lot tougher than it looks. The moral here is that observation is *one* way to learn, but not a complete method in itself.)

***

Conversation is another good way to learn from people, and we can learn through chitchat. You might think that learning from conversations is pretty disorganized or random; however, most people are quite skilled at consciously or unconsciously shaping conversations to provide useful or interesting information. For one thing, if we're not interested in a topic, we tend to tune out, leaving the speaker chattering away to him or herself, or we change the topic to something that truly interests us. Thus we are constantly casting out "nets" of conversation, dredging up ideas from other people.

Most of us also use conversation as a way to test out our ideas with other people, so even as we share our own ideas and information, we're listening with half an ear to the feedback the other person is giving us: Is what I'm saying making sense?

A more direct way of learning from people is through *lectures* or *demonstrations*. In simple terms, these are methods people use to tell directly what they know. As you get farther along in school, you'll

✳ ✳ ✳ QUESTING ✳ ✳ ✳

As an experiment, list some of the people with whom you've had conversations today. What have you learned? Can you remember any ways in which you "bent" the conversation to get answers to your own questions? Did you shift the topic onto familiar ground? Have you shared any bright new ideas with others today?

or

Eavesdrop!

That's right. Listen in on a few conversations. Listen to people chatting at the mall or at a fast food restaurant. What are they discussing? What kind of ideas and information are they sharing? How do they answer each other's questions? What are they learning from one another? What do *you* learn from them? Write your observations in the Learner's Notebook.

probably have more classes in which teachers give lectures and you take notes on the information being presented. Listening to school lectures is not terribly popular with students, but it's a good way to get a lot of information fast. You may also find that there are some public lectures given around your town. Check a schedule in your newspaper or at the library. You'll find people lecturing on everything from new books to theories of space travel.

Demonstrations, like lectures, center on somebody passing information directly by showing some of the skills he or she has gained. Again, you can check the paper or the community calendar at the library to find some demonstrations around town: how to use diving gear, how to make things with home workshop equipment, an introduction to the martial arts, how to sew, what to look for in an all-terrain vehicle.

In addition, television has daily lectures and demonstrations.

Check the TV schedule. Public television—the educational chan-nel—is particularly good at supplying demonstrations. You may also find that public access channels on cable TV carry presentations by people in your community, people you can meet in person if their demonstrations interested you.

While lectures and demonstrations provide for a direct transfer of knowledge from one person to another, *tutoring* or *coaching* helps you learn to do it yourself. Earlier I mentioned learning to ride a bicycle. A famous philosopher, Michael Polanyi, has observed that there's no way you can learn to ride a bike by listening to somebody tell you how to do it. To learn, you have to climb on the bike, turn the pedals, take a few falls, and figure it out for yourself.

However, it helps tremendously to have somebody there to help tutor or coach you when you're learning to ride a bike, somebody who can assist you in getting started, who can tell you what you're doing wrong, who can offer some support and encouragement (and maybe tape a Band-Aid on your scratched knee). Most people learn quite rapidly from a skilled coach, who can give us the information we need when we need it. If the problem with your bicycling is that you're not pedaling hard enough, you don't need a lecture or a dem-onstration on how the pedals work; you need somebody to say, "Pump harder!"

Who are the people from whom you can learn in your town or city? Figure 5-1 suggests just a few of the possibilities.

Interviewing

Observation, conversation, lectures, demonstrations, coaching, tutor-ing. These are methods that each of us uses almost every day to learn from others. There is also a special method of searching for informa-tion borrowed from journalism, where the *interview* is an especially valuable way to learn. You might think that interviewing is simply a matter of getting in touch with somebody and then asking a few ques-tions, but there's more to it than that. People often enjoy being inter-

----

FIGURE 5-1:   Who Are the People in Your Neighborhood?

Some of the people from whom you can learn in most towns and cities.

Accountant	Airplane pilot	Advertising writer
Allergist	Ambulance driver	Agriculturalist
Architect	Baker	Beekeeper
Bill collector	Biologist	Bricklayer
Butcher	Cab driver	Cabinetmaker
Cardiologist	Chef	City planner
Computer programmer	Copy writer	Day care worker
Dentist	Detective	Dietician
Disc jockey	Draftsman	Dry cleaner
Electrician	Engineer	Exterminator
Family doctor	Farmer	Film developer
Fire chief	Flight attendant	Forester
Furniture repairer	Gas inspector	Geologist
Golf pro	Groundskeeper	Gunsmith
Health agent	Home economist	Horse trainer
Hospital worker	Illustrator	Immunologist
Insurance agent	Jeweler	Judge
Kennel attendant	Kitchen helper	Land agent
Landscaper	Lawyer	Librarian
Lifeguard	Mathematician	Meter reader
Movie critic	Musician	Newscaster
Optician	Organist	Park ranger
Payroll clerk	Pianist	Police chief
Quality control tester	Radiologist	Referee
Riveter	Safety inspector	Salesperson
Secretary	Shipping clerk	Soils analyst
Tailor	Teacher	TV engineer
Undertaker	Veterinarian	Waiter/waitress
Warehouse clerk	Water analyst	Welder
Well driller	Winemaker	Writer
X-ray technician	Yogi	Zoologist

----

viewed, but they don't have time to waste and will want you to be well organized and get directly to the point.

"Who are the people in your neighborhood?" goes a Sesame Street song that you've probably heard hundreds of times. Figure 5-1 suggests some of the specialists and experts you'll find in almost every town in America, large or small. All of these people are knowledgeable and can answer many of your questions. You can reach many of them by telephone, though I personally find it much more interesting and productive to do interviews in person.

In Chapter 2 I discussed question asking and showed you some ways to narrow down the questions you want to ask. Use that skill in planning an interview. Ask yourself:

> What is this person's special area of interest or knowledge? What is she most likely to know or want to talk about?
> Which of the questions I want answered is he likely to be able to answer?

Make yourself two lists, the "first string" or major questions that you want to ask, and some backups of lesser importance, just in case your interviewee doesn't talk as much as you wanted. I recommend that you practice asking your questions to family members or friends *before* going to the interview, just to make certain you know what you want to ask and that you'll be understood.

Think, too, about phrasing your questions so that they get the information you want, and don't insult or irritate the interviewee. Try to avoid asking what are called "loaded" questions. *Don't* ask the president of a company, "How come your products are junk?" More tactfully (and less loaded) ask, "I've heard that you have some problems with quality control. Will you comment on that?" Don't ask the mayor, "How come you don't do anything for kids in after-school programs?" Do say, "I'm interested in learning about after-school programs sponsored by the city. Can you tell me about what you're doing?"

Bring a notepad with your questions to the interview, and have plenty of blank paper to write answers. Most interviewers nowadays also carry along a cassette recorder and tape the whole interview, thus saving themselves writing time. Ask the person's permission to tape, and if he or she says something that you think you'd like to quote directly, write it down on the spot, making certain that you have it accurately.

Sharpen your pencils before you go on the interview; check the cassette recorder to make certain the batteries are fresh, and doublecheck to see that you have a tape inside, one that will last long enough to record the whole interview.

Remember all the politeness rules in interviewing: be on time; be courteous; don't stay too long; say thank you. I also like to follow up interviews by writing the person a short note of appreciation.

The other follow-up to a good interview is to review the notes or tapes as soon as possible. Head for your learning center when you get home and look over your notes. If you're like me, you probably wrote in some sort of shorthand, with lots of arrows and abbreviations. Now's the time to write those notes out in detail so you won't forget what they mean. Listen to the tape and copy down any important statements that your interviewee made (or, if there are parts of the tape that are murky, you might have to write a follow-up letter asking for clarification).

Sometimes an interview will form the basis of a whole paper or report for school; sometimes it will be part of a broader base of research that you are doing. In either case, learn how to interview and become successful at it. No matter how you plan to further your education, or no matter what career you choose, skill as an interviewer will come in very handy.

Surveys and Polls

Check your daily newspaper. The chances are quite good that you'll find a survey of one sort or another in the news, sports, or business section. You may learn from the TV page that the Nielsen ratings are

---

* * * QUESTING * * *

Look through the many **Quest** topics that you've put in your Learner's Notebook (or make a list of the topics that you're currently interested in, either in school or around home). Which of those topics might be good ones to study through interviews? Jot down some of the questions and practice asking them, to a friend, a parent, or to your tape recorder. You might even want to get somebody to roleplay a possible interviewee so you can practice your skills. Work up your nerve. (It's not easy to do an interview, and even professional reporters sometimes get nervous before they go out to do one.) Make an appointment to see one of your interviewees, and do it! After you've finished the whole experience, write an assessment of how it went. In what ways do you feel you could sharpen your interview skills?

Then go do it again!

---

up or down for a popular show—the Nielsen is simply a poll of a selected group of television viewers to discover what they're watching. You may find a phone-in poll, where readers have called the paper to record their opinions. You may see the results of a poll showing that the president's popularity is rising or falling, or that people think their congressional representatives should vote one way or another, or that the fans think a basketball coach should be kept or fired.

You can conduct polls and surveys of your own to unlock people's ideas and opinions. You'll find, too, that many people enjoy being polled and will readily fill out a form or answer a few questions in a survey.

What sort of information can you collect? Through polls you might find out things as diverse as:

· who people think will be the league champion in sports

· whether they think the government is handling foreign affairs well
· favorite jokes
· childhood games or myths
· how to: make an omelette, unstick a zipper, sew on a button

It's important to note that most polls ask for people to give opinions, rather than to state facts. That, in turn, creates a problem of accuracy and reliability.

There's a story that goes the rounds in advertising agencies. Years ago a company polled beer drinkers about whether they like light or regular beer. The pollsters learned that people claimed to prefer light by about 8 to 1. But in fact, regular beer was the best seller by just about the same 8 to 1 margin. People were not exactly lying about their preferences, but because they thought one kind of beer sounded fashionable, they tended to list it as a preference, even though they didn't drink it.

Or to take another example: just before celebrating its hundredth anniversary, the Coca-Cola Company thought it was time for a change and field tested a new flavor of Coke. In blind taste tests (where people didn't know what they were drinking) pollsters found that people preferred the new flavor. With much fanfare, the company brought out its "new" Coke. To its dismay, however, many Coke drinkers refused to buy the new product and demanded a return to the original. After just a few months Coca-Cola reintroduced its older "classic" formula. In this case, the poll—the blind taste test—was probably reliable, but in real life, people don't drink with blindfolds on. They buy a product for a number of different reasons, including nostalgia.

All this is by way of saying that as you poll or survey people, you must be very cautious about interpreting results.

Designing a Survey

The first step is to figure out what you want to know and what sort of information people can give you. There are no set rules for this; the best way to learn about it is to develop a survey of your own.

* * * SURVEY QUEST—PART I * * *

Take a topic you're interested knowing more about—rockets, computers, mathematics, magazines, television, political events, school, church, home, newspapers, pets and animals, the future, the past, tomorrow, yesterday. . . . In your Learner's Notebook make a list of the information you'd like to obtain. For instance, you might collect people's opinions on:

· the space program and how it's going
· how they use computers in their daily lives
· whether or not they like math
· the magazines they read regularly
· the television programs they prefer
· what they think about recent political events

Once you've picked a general area of information you want to obtain, create *sub*questions or topics that you could develop in your poll. For example, if the space program was on your mind, you might poll people about:

· where they think it will be going in coming years
· how the U.S. program stacks up against that of the Soviet Union
· whether or not they'd like to go into space
· whether they think their children or grandchildren will ever fly in space

Actually, even those subtopics can sometimes be divided further. If you were focusing just on the *success* of the program you might want to find out what people think about:

· rocket accidents and the deaths of astronauts
· specific space launches they've seen on TV
· whether they think space travel is safe

Fill a page or two of your notebook with topics that you'd like to quiz people about. Then proceed to Survey **Quest**—Part II, a few pages farther on in this chapter.

You can collect information for your poll by simply going to the street (or to school or to your friends or family) with notebook and pencil in hand and to ask people's opinions on matters, jotting down replies. However, for accuracy and consistency, many pollsters duplicate a list of questions for all their respondents to answer. That way you can be certain that each person is reacting to the same questions.

There are a number of ways in which you can design questionnaires or surveys, and you've probably seen many of them in magazines. For example, you may select a *short answer* survey or questionnaire. Here you simply list your questions and leave some space for people to reply.

QUESTION: Do you think that the U.S. space program has been successful on the whole?

ANSWER: (Leave room for them to write in an answer.)

These short answers will give you a lot of information, but you may want data that you can calculate more conveniently, something that will give you a number like: 25 percent of people surveyed think the space program is a success. In that case you might prefer to use an *agree/disagree* questionnaire:

INSTRUCTIONS: Indicate how strongly you agree or disagree with the following statements by circling your response.

America's space program is a success

Strongly Agree	Agree	No Opinion	Disagree	Strongly Disagree

With that format, you can come up with some figures such as: "22 out of 30 people polled strongly agree that the space program has been a success."

If you don't need exact numbers, you might give people a *free association* test:

INSTRUCTIONS: Write down whatever comes into your mind about the following words:

Outer Space

(Leave room for a reply.)

Rocket Safety

(Leave room for a reply.)

Still another form that people seem to enjoy doing is the *matchup* questionnaire:

INSTRUCTIONS: Match the first names of astronauts in Column A with their last names in Column B.

A		B
John	_____	McAuliffe
Sally	_____	Ride
Virgil	_____	Armstrong
Neil	_____	Grissom
Christa	_____	Glenn

Or you could do your poll as a multiple choice questionnaire:

INSTRUCTIONS: Choose the correct answer to each of the following questions.

Neil Armstrong was the first American to:
a. fly in outer space
b. be killed in a space accident
c. walk on the moon
d. go to Mars

* * * SURVEY QUEST—PART II * * *

You've seen several different ways to create a survey. Each style will get you different kinds of answers. Look at the list of topics you created in Survey **Quest**—Part I. Now experiment with putting them into a poll. Which format will work best for you? Of course, you don't have to be limited in your choice of items. Your poll could contain free association, short answers, multiple choice, matching, and agree/disagree. But don't make it so complicated that people are confused by it.

Experiment with creating a variety of questions for a poll you'd like to give. Then *field test* it by trying your questions on a few friends. If they are confused by any items, rewrite them. Also look at the answers you are getting from people. Are they telling you what you want to know? If not, rework the questionnaire some more. (Then go on to Survey **Quest**—Part III.)

An especially important aspect of polling is selecting people to participate. Professional pollsters are scientific in selecting what's called a "sampling" or "sample population." In the Nielsen TV ratings, for example, much effort goes into choosing the people to be polled to ensure that they are a "representative sample" of all TV viewers in a particular area. For most of your polls, you don't need to be quite so scientific and can simply ask people you encounter in your daily travels: friends, parents, schoolmates, etc. Sometimes if your teachers know you are conducting a poll, they'll let you administer it to the whole class, which will give you twenty-five or thirty answers right away.

✳ ✳ ✳ SURVEY QUEST—PART III ✳ ✳ ✳

Do it!

Make some copies of your questionnaire. Photocopy them, recopy them by hand, run off copies on a computer printer, or get some carbon paper and make duplicates. How many will be enough? Newspaper polls often include a thousand or more informants. For most of your polls, ten to twenty people will be sufficient. (But wouldn't it be fun to poll everybody in your school—maybe three or four hundred kids or more?)

Then collect your data to make sense of it. Sort through all the questionnaires. Add up the numbers. Jot down the most interesting or informative short answers and free associations. At this point you'll do something called "eyeballing" your data, poring over it until it makes sense to you and you can see patterns.

There will be more on ways of figuring out what it means in Chapter 7, Learning from Research.

Still More Ways to Learn from People

Television

Much of TV is filled with violent shows or silly situation comedies or soap operas that aren't very challenging to the mind. However, television gives you an easy way to learn from people. In addition to educational shows and demonstrations, you'll find specials, dramas, and films on the tube, many of which will fit right into your learning **Quests**.

The *nightly news,* for example, gives you a view of what has been going on in the world; it allows you to learn from many different people: the anchorperson, the correspondents, the people who are interviewed in connection with various news stories. *Documentaries* do just what the title implies—they document or provide data on important events and issues around the world, presenting film and interviews to help the viewer understand things more fully. There are also *interviews* conducted on television, and a popular feature on many stations is the *magazine* show, which provides information on a wide range of topics. Even *talk shows* give you a chance to learn from others.

To tune in on television as a learning source, make it a habit to scan the newspaper viewer's guide each week, marking down the shows that you think would be interesting to watch. If you have a video recorder, you can even tape some of the shows for study at a more convenient time.

If you have cable TV, also make it a habit to scan the public access channels that are run by schools, colleges, and public service agencies. You'll find a wide range of community affairs programs on cable TV.

Video and Audio Cassettes

Much interesting information is now available on cassettes. You can watch famous actors and actresses do their exercise programs, and you can listen to inspirational speakers tell you how to better your life. If your time for reading is limited, you can purchase taped copies of books and listen to them on your Walkman as you stroll about your daily business. You may wish to own some cassettes, but increasingly they are available on loan from libraries or for an inexpensive rental fee in video and audio stores.

Performances

Small and large towns all over the country have a range of "shows": concerts, lectures, plays, art exhibits, photographic displays. Check your local newspaper to learn what's available. In larger towns and cities, there may even be a monthly or quarterly magazine that tells what's going on.

✳ ✳ ✳ QUESTING ✳ ✳ ✳

Create yet another new section of your Learner's Notebook— Coming Events. Once each week, check the TV program guide and the community calendar and make a list of forthcoming events that will help you learn what you want to know. You may not be able to get to everything you'd like to see or do, but at least make certain you know what's going on.

The Telephone

Alexander Graham Bell's invention is a superb learning tool. If you're puzzled over some factual information or need to know the title of a book, you can call your library reference desk and save yourself a trip. You can phone business and government offices to gain information, and you can tap into weather lines, news lines, movie information, and community calendars on the phone.

Long distance costs extra money, but you may want to use it occasionally to extend your learning. The phone allows you to speak with people in other parts of the country, perhaps experts in business or industry or people well known for their skills in one of your hobby areas.

You can also make some long-distance calls free. Many businesses have toll-free numbers, chiefly to let people order products, but also as a service to consumers—to answer their questions. Check at your local library for a directory of toll-free numbers. You can also find

✳ ✳ ✳ COMPUTERQUEST ✳ ✳ ✳

The computer offers some exciting new ways of getting in touch with people. Computer bulletin boards combine the speed and efficiency of the telephone with the advantages of letter writing. A number of people can participate in a bulletin board "conversation" all at once. You type in a question you want answered and people who are "on line" provide answers. You can also "post" your question and come back to the bulletin board later to see how people have answered it. A number of bulletin boards have been created for special interest groups like bicycle riders or computer users. As you use a bulletin board, you get to "know" people who participate regularly, and you can become computer pen pals.

If your (or your school's) computer has a *modem* you can become involved with a bulletin board group. The telephone numbers of these groups are published in computer magazines and in special directories that you can find at the library. One caution: If a bulletin board is outside your town, you may have to call long distance to use it. Those long distance fees mount up very quickly, and for many people, long distance bulletin boards become prohibitively expensive.

For more information on all these possibilities, do some **Questing** with the people who are experts in your town: the folks who run the computer store, the members of a local computer club, the people at your school who are computer buffs or "hackers." Ask them to help you get hooked into the bulletin boards in your area.

out if a particular company has a toll-free number by dialing 1-800-555-1212. Naturally, you don't want to abuse the service by calling with no purpose, but if you have legitimate questions—about computers, cars, consumer products—you can get your answers by toll-free long distance.

Letters

For the price of a first-class stamp you can send a letter anywhere in North America. For a few cents more, you can send a letter any place in the world. Granted, letters are slower than telephoning, but in the end they are often more efficient and far less expensive. You can write letters to politicians, rock or movie stars, editors of magazines and newspapers, government information sources, experts in your hobby, authors of books or articles, public relations departments in business and industry, catalog supply houses, and public and community service agencies. Keep a supply of stamps in your learning center and remind yourself that a letter will often bring you a wealth of information in reply.

The Community of Learners

So who are the people in your neighborhood? In this chapter I've tried to show you that human beings are an amazing source of information. And your "neighborhood" truly is the world: with the use of phones, letters, and computers you can make contact with people all over the globe as a way of enhancing your knowledge. You are truly a member of a worldwide community of learners.

6 Learning from Places

The building where I have my office at Michigan State University is named Morrill Hall, after Justin Morrill, a U.S. senator, who, in the middle of the last century, created some land grant colleges. The senator arranged to give the states large parcels of land that they could use to build and finance schools designed specifically to help the people learn practical skills like farming. Michigan State University was originally Michigan *Agricultural* College, and among the oldest buildings on campus is a monument to Justin Morrill: the hall that bears his name.

In the university archives we've found a photograph that shows Morrill Hall seventy-five years ago, when it was still new and the campus roads were dirt rather than asphalt. In those days Morrill Hall was a women's dormitory, and what is now a parking lot was then a duck pond.

Morrill Hall is rich in history. At one time, it was the college infirmary for students who were ill or injured, and a room in the basement is still known by some of the old-timers as the "nurse's room," even though the infirmary moved out years ago. The building was once covered with ivy, but ten years ago the ivy was torn off to save money when the university was in financial trouble, a bleak era in our history.

In some English department offices, you will find a portable chain ladder rolled up in a bookcase, and another story can be told about the building's history. Morrill Hall was built without fire escapes, and the faculty members were supplied with these chain ladders, so that in the event of a fire, they could climb out third and fourth floor windows and scale down the outside walls to safety. Now there is a massive fire escape on the west side of the building where the ivy once grew.

Still another era in history is revealed by the basement entrance, which was remodeled recently to eliminate stairs and provide access for wheelchairs. That entrance is a kind of monument to the perseverance of the handicapped in obtaining their right to access.

Once upon a time, Morrill Hall housed the faculty of education; it now provides offices for professors of philosophy, English, history, and a newfangled department known as "learning services."

Thus, you can learn much of the history of Michigan State University just by studying a building like Morrill Hall and learning its stories. Morrill Hall is an example of what this chapter is all about: learning from, by, and about *places*.

But there's more to learning from places than just ivy and architecture. Inside Morrill Hall are books and libraries, coffee pots and computer terminals, professors and students. If you have a question to ask on almost any subject, there's probably somebody there who can either answer it directly, look up the answer, or tell you where to go within the university to find an answer.

Institutions—or places—are interesting as buildings, but they are more interesting because of their human resources, the people who work (and worked) or play (and played) there.

The world is filled with places where you can learn. You can go to the Boston Garden to see great basketball being played by the Celtics, but it's also a place where you can absorb the feelings and stories and legends that go way back in basketball history. You can go to Stanley Park in Vancouver, British Columbia, to learn the history of the Kwakiutl Indians and to see examples of their art in totem pole carvings. You can go to the Museum of Science and Industry in Chicago to study the history of industry in America or to the Ontario Science Center in Toronto, Ontario, to explore scientific discoveries with your "hands on." You can go to Chinatown in San Francisco or Los Angeles or Chicago or New York to learn about Chinese people and customs, and you can visit Bourbon Street in New Orleans to learn about the history and art of jazz. You can even go to an amusement park like Disneyland or Six Flags or Busch Gardens and learn a surprising amount about the world in which we live.

However, you don't have to travel to theme parks or large cities to find places where you can learn. At the hardware store in your town, you can learn to repair things; at the travel agency you can learn about seeing the world or your state; at the office of the mayor you can learn about the rules and regulations of your town. The creaky old merry-go-round at the county fairgrounds can tell you stories if you know how to look for them, and the local donut shop is a place where you can learn—about baking or about world affairs—if you know how to ask questions or just plain listen.

For just about as long as people have lived in social groups and formed communities, they have created places or institutions to store and share information, products, services, and ideas. Every place has a history—even that brand-new fast food restaurant going in at the mall—and the history of a place tells you something about what people have learned and found valuable over the years. You can learn from any place you visit, whether by studying the place itself and how it's put together or by talking with the people who congregate there.

Schools

Practically as soon as they had settled on the shores of New England, the colonists passed a law that every town of fifty households must establish schools for the purpose of teaching children to read and write. Schools are deeply woven into the fabric of American history. Except for your home, you will probably spend more time in school than in any other place in the next few years.

It's pretty obvious to point out that schools are places where you can learn, and you might suspect that now I'm going to give a little pep talk about being a good student and hitting your books hard. That's not bad advice, but I want to help you see that there's a lot more to school than just books and homework assignments.

Edgar Friedenberg, a sociologist studying how people work and live together, once described an "ideal" student, Stanley. In his book, *The Vanishing Adolescent,* Friedenberg reports that Stanley used the school as you would a train or plane schedule: he looked around, studied what would be of most use to him, and then "climbed aboard" those activities and learning experiences that would take him where he wanted to go in life. Stanley talked with teachers after class about their experiences and his own curiosities, not to raise his grades or become a teacher's pet, but because he was interested. He joined the after-school clubs that interested him and ignored the ones he thought were silly. Stanley was a careful consumer of educational services.

It's common to find students who are loaded with school spirit, who are enthusiastic supporters of sports and other activities. It's also quite common to find students who are bored by their studies and wish they were someplace else. What's unusual is to find a young learner who realizes that school is a good place to learn beyond what's required in class and who takes full advantage of what's there.

To begin learning more from your schoolplace, look to the teachers, who can be a gold mine of education and interests. Your teachers can do more than help you with your math or spelling. They can tell you about history, art, music, science, travel, sports, hobbies, and the world in general. The trick is to ask them questions, to find out what they're excited about and what they have to say that will help you with your own learning.

When you're assigned a report or project, you'll probably go to the library to find some books and other materials that will help you (see Chapter 4). But remember about learning from people (see Chapter 5). Look around the school to see who might be interviewed or who might have some tips and pointers on where to go for research materials. (Tell your plans to the teacher who assigned the project. Most teachers will allow you to get help from people as well as books, but sometimes this sort of help is ruled out of order.)

School learning need not be limited to the teachers. You can talk with the principal and the counselors, and the custodians, technicians, and dieticians have things to tell and teach you. You can also involve yourself in extracurricular activities: sports, music, art, clubs. You can even start up a club of fellow learners if you don't find your own interests represented in your school. (See the Appendix for ideas on starting a **Questars** club.)

What I'm suggesting, then, is that you regard school as an opportunity to explore and discover, not just a chore. School can be a good place for you to exercise what teachers call "intellectual curiosity," the drive to know more, to be excited by a wide range of ideas, not limited to what you find in the textbooks you're assigned to study.

Other Institutions of Learning

"Institutions of learning" is kind of an off-putting phrase, isn't it? I'm using it simply to suggest that your learning doesn't have to be limited to the particular school you attend. Around your town there are probably several schools you can use to learn more about your special interests.

The chances are good that you can take advantage of a *college* or *university* nearby, perhaps a huge "multiversity" of many thousands of students, possibly a local or community college with just a few hundred students. Even though you're not enrolled as a student, you can often make use of the college's learning resources. Some colleges open their libraries to the community. There are professors in most

---

* * * QUESTING * * *

What can you learn from your school?

What are your favorite subjects? How can you learn *more* in them than what's required to pass the tests? Which subjects do you like least? Think about ways you could do a little extra reading and study in that area or get some extra help from the teacher. Talk to your teachers about their interests and hobbies. What books do your teachers like to read? What do they do in their spare time? (But don't intrude on your teacher's personal life.) Most teachers will welcome your questions if they understand you're interested in learning.

Go to your school library and spend some time discovering what you hadn't noticed before, especially the human resources. Talk to the librarian. Tell him or her about your interests and hobbies and see if there are some new books or magazines that would be valuable to read.

Find out about after-school clubs and organizations. Is there a science club? a computer club? a young writer's workshop? a soccer team? Will the librarian sponsor a **Questars** club? Which of the school's activities interest you most? Join up!

---

colleges who can answer your questions on everything from rocketry to taking care of your goldfish. A few of the profs may seem a bit crabby and would prefer spending time in the laboratory to talking, but you'll also find that a great many are delighted to meet with a young person who is genuinely interested in learning.

Don't be bashful about picking up the phone and calling your local college or university. There is often a college switchboard or information service that can help you get the right numbers to call.

Many colleges also run special activities for learners your age. My own university sponsors manuscript days for young writers, after-school **Questars** clubs, art workshops, dance programs, children's theater, science competition, computer clubs, and tutoring services for people having trouble with reading or mathematics. You can use the university during the regular school year, or you can come stay for a week or so as part of a summer camp. High school students can even take college courses for credit, which, if you're doing well in your classes, may be just the thing to extend your learning and interests.

If there isn't a college campus close enough for you to reach easily, you can look for *extension* courses offered in your town, courses that the college offers away from its main campus. Once you know where the extension classes are given in your town, you might be able to meet with a professor before or after class, or even sit in on a session to see what's going on.

Business and *training* colleges may also be helpful to you. These are schools that specialize in preparing people for particular jobs. If you're having difficulty with your grammar or spelling, you can often call a secretarial college for assistance. If you'd like to know more about electronics, check the resources at a nearby technical college. You'll find that many communities have schools or colleges that teach driving (either a car or a truck), beauty and hairdressing, broadcasting, modeling, medical assistance, and legal aid.

Many public school systems supplement their services with *community* and *adult education* programs. If you check these out, you may find yourself taking a class in bicycle maintenance, gardening, cartooning, first aid, swimming, or underwater diving. Ask at your school board offices for a calendar of upcoming courses, or keep an eye on your community newspaper, which will probably publish a schedule from time to time.

Many educators hold the ideal of developing a "lifelong learning habit" in their students. They hope that after you've left their classes and graduated from school, you'll continue learning. You can begin developing that habit right now by discovering those other institutions of learning in your town and taking advantage of them.

```
* * * QUESTING * * *

Look in your phone book yellow pages under "Schools." Jot
down the addresses of schools or colleges that you think might
be helpful to you at some time in the future. Call a local college
and ask about the programs they run for people your age. If you
have a question about teeth or hair or the law or medical
emergencies, call the appropriate training college and ask your
questions.
```

Learning Through the Government

"Your tax dollars at work" is a phrase you'll see posted from time to time when government agencies are at work repairing roads, building new offices, creating a park or playground. Most young learners are not taxpayers in the fullest sense—you probably pay sales tax on things you buy, but you're not making enough money from your paper route to pay state or federal income tax. Nevertheless, your parents are taxpayers, and you have access to a great many services and information sources through the government. Not all these services are as obvious as repaving a road or plowing snow, so you need to learn to look for them.

Right around town, for example, your *local government* has a surprising number of resources available. The city clerk's office can tell you about voting procedures, licensing a dog, or registering your bicycle. The zoning office can help you understand how new businesses and industries come to your town. The public works department can describe the source of your water supply and how the town disposes of sewage and trash. The mayor's office can answer questions about the city's plans for development, recreation, and education. Call the parks department to find out about programs for people your age, and visit the school department or superintendent's office to learn about adult education programs.

The next rung up on the governmental ladder is the *county,* whose "seat"—or main offices—may or may not be close by. If you can't go directly to the county building by bus or bike, you can use the omni-purpose telephone to request materials and information. The resources offered by county governments vary widely, but you may be able to locate information on such topics as court procedures, civil defense, community mental health, agricultural extension, economic development, animal control, health care, care for the aged, and library services.

County offices are an especially good resource if you are interested in community or family history. You can track down the history of old buildings and streets, learn about community leaders of yesteryear, even do research into your own family tree (if your family started out where you live).

With both local and county governments, the telephone book is your best guide and resource. Look up the name of your town or county and you'll find a long list of offices. Don't just ring up offices for the fun of it. Instead, think about questions you'd like to have answered. Government officials are busy, but they are a part of your tax dollars at work and you have a right to request information and services from them.

The *state* government is the next step up that ladder of government, and you may be astounded to discover the number of services available. I'm lucky enough to live just a few miles from the state capital of Michigan, so it's easy for me to take advantage of state services. I can either drive to offices or make a local phone call. However, even if you live hundreds of miles from the capital, there are many ways you can draw on state resources by mail or phone (sometimes toll-free).

At your local library, find the phone book for the city in which your state capital is located. (You may be able to find this information at the local office of your state representative or senator.) Look up the state government and copy down the addresses and phone numbers of offices that might prove helpful. Sometimes you'll find there are toll-free numbers you can call in the capital city for information on tourism or business and industry. Otherwise, use a letter to seek information. (Sometimes, too, you can drop off requests at the local office of your state legislator.)

Your state can provide you with information on crime control, the lottery, commerce, travel, energy, geology, natural resources, education, animals and agriculture, aviation, civil defense, military affairs, parks, libraries, and hundreds of other topics.

The *federal* or *national* government is the final level. One of the most valuable learning resources maintained by the U.S. government is our national parks and monuments program. Whenever you travel, check the maps and tourism guides. You'll find everything from national monuments and parks to wildlife preserves and refuges.

The post office is a federal service that gives you access to your government. Especially helpful is the *Consumer Information Catalog,* which you can get free by writing the Consumer Information Center, P. O. Box 100, Pueblo, Colorado 81002. This booklet is published every few months and lists hundreds of leaflets and brochures that you can get free or for a small charge. Through the federal government you can learn how to improve your test-taking skills, start a business, protect your home from thieves or fire, control your diet, grow food, control acne, buy public land cheap, find a campsite, start a stamp collection, and program a computer.

Writing your representatives in the U.S. Senate and House of Representatives is a good habit to develop, too. As you read your newspaper, think about important state and national issues and write to your elected officials expressing your opinion.

Museums, Galleries, Exhibits

Some institutions are organized especially to help people learn. At a museum you'll find materials displayed for you to study, often with labels and explanations that answer your questions. You can do research at a museum or gallery, too. If you're working on a school report, a museum near you may have an exhibit that will save you time reading and give you a deeper understanding of your topic.

You may be surprised at the number of museums near you, especially small or specialized museums. Within ten miles of my home are a state history museum, two old schoolhouse museums, a "hands on" science museum, several art galleries, a restored historic township, a planetarium, an old car museum, a "living steam" museum (with steam-driven farm tractors), a women's history museum, and—believe it or not—a tuba museum. As I said, I'm lucky to be near a state capital and a large university, both of which help supply these museums, but there are many, many museums in smaller places, too. Almost every county has a historical museum, and you'll find all kinds of museums and displays as you travel, ranging from curiosities like a seashell museum (featuring an alleged man-eating clam) to museums commemorating the dominant industry of the area (like a steam shovel museum in a mining town!).

Exhibits are minimuseums that you'll find in many different locations. The airport near me has a display called the "Freedom Shrine" with copies of famous documents in American history: the Declaration of Independence, the Bill of Rights, and others. While waiting for luggage to arrive, you can spend a few minutes studying these artifacts of history.

Many state highway departments have displays of regional history or industry at roadside rest areas, and you can learn about the territory through which you are traveling. You'll also find exhibits of community interest in bank lobbies and in display cases at the office of the city clerk. There are traveling exhibits that may come to your town: displays on health, history, the military, music, and art. A circus or carnival is an exhibit of a kind, and don't miss your county fair, which is rich in demonstrations and displays. Often collectors of objects will get together for shows, and from time to time people in your community may show off their bottles, model railroads, or old cars. Keep your eyes open then, not only for displays and exhibits around town, but for word in the newspaper about coming events.

You can even find displays in commercial locations, displays that are designed to *sell,* but can be used to *learn.* Visit antique stores nearby and you'll discover a different kind of "museum," preserving objects that are a part of history and culture. A jewelry store will have a variety of displays from which you can learn about valuable gems and stones, precious metals, and timekeeping. Hardware stores are "how to" museums, and department stores can be considered "museums" of furniture and fashions. If you want to buy a new bike, visit bike stores where you'll see all the competing brands lined up for comparison and inspection. Frequently malls have specialized shows: antiques, home construction, automobiles. Use those displays as you would a museum to learn more about a topic of interest.

Study exhibits, galleries, and museums with an active and curious imagination. Too often people simply soak up the sights or remark on the odd things they've seen. Ask yourself some questions to get more out of displays than you might ordinarily:

> What does this display tell me about the life and interests of the person who created it? (People make or create objects to serve a purpose, and you can figure out what people were like by looking at the objects they make.)
>
> What can I learn about how things are made? (For example, you can learn a lot about an artist's techniques by studying a painting close up.)
>
> How can I apply this in my own life? (You may be surprised to discover that long ago, people had figured out good ways of solving problems that we sometimes think are unique.)

Commerce and Community

This chapter may seem rather like an ad for the telephone company, but the yellow pages of your phone book can provide you with access to one of the greatest learning resources: the businesses (and business people) in your town. Whether you live in a small town with just a

```
* * * QUESTING * * *

Look in the phone book yellow pages to learn about museums
and displays near you. Check under "museums." You can also
write or call your state's tourism office or the automobile club to
ask for a travel brochure that lists places to visit around your
state. In addition to museums, exhibits, and galleries, you'll find
listings of old homes and businesses that have been restored and
are open for public viewing. Keep a sharp eye out for exhibits
like art fairs, festivals, and celebrations, where people bring
crafts and art to display and sell.
```

few businesses or a major city with thousands, you can use the phone
book to find learning resources. A note inside my phone book asks:

Want to buy something?
Need a service?
Want to rent something?
Want to sell something?
Looking for professional people?
Want a brand-name product?

All these needs can be met through the yellow pages, which will often
include maps of your area and a listing of transportation services you
can use to get where you're going.

What can you learn from your community? For some ideas, see
Figure 6-1.

FIGURE 6-1: Commerce and Community

Visit	To Learn
Factory	How products are made, who makes them, what skills are involved, how people prepare for careers.

Movie theater	How films are booked, the tastes of people in your town, how theaters make money.
Clothing store	What's new in fashion, how clothing is mass produced, where clothes come from.
County agent's office	The principal agricultural products of your area, how things are grown and marketed, problems facing farmers.
Hunting/fishing club	What animals are hunted and why, how people find game, how they feel about hunting and fishing, the best fishing spots in your area.
Historical society	The history of your town.
Employment commission	The kinds of jobs available in your area, how people train for them, the problems with unemployment in your region.
Chamber of commerce	What's being done to attract people to your town, what businesses are thriving.
Any small business	How business people feel about owning their own business, how they learned to do it, the future of small businesses.
Farm market	What agricultural products are sold, which come from your area and which are imported, how farmers do business during the off season.
Law office	The services provided, how to get a lawyer when you need one, how much legal services cost, how to become a lawyer.
Piano shop	How pianos are tuned, how they are made and repaired, how to tell a good one from a poor one.
Housing office	How much new housing is being built in your town, how people go about building new living quarters, problems with housing.
Hospital	How emergencies are handled, why hospitals are expensive, how they are organized, careers in health care.

Detective agency	What non-TV detectives do, how they are trained, how they spend their time, whether they carry guns, how they use a lie detector.
Dentist's office	New directions in dentistry, painless dentistry, careers in dental health.
Baker	How to bake, how to measure.
Beauty parlor	New fashions, what hair stylists know, how they are trained, who uses a beauty salon.
VFW (Veterans of Foreign Wars) post	Who from your community has fought overseas, what war is like, what veterans feel about defense and wars and peace.
Radio/TV studio	How broadcasts are sent out, how TV/radio stations make money, how employees are trained.
Newspaper	Everything from how news is gathered to how it is written to how it is edited to how it is printed to how the papers are distributed.

✳ ✳ ✳ QUESTING ✳ ✳ ✳

Go back to some of the lists of questions and topics you prepared in your Learner's Notebook after reading Chapter 2. Survey (and perhaps add to) your list of questions worth asking. Then open the phone book to the yellow pages and flip through from A to Z, looking for places in your community where you might find answers. Start using the resources of commerce and community in your **Questing.**

Civic and Charitable Organizations

Organizations and clubs are not precisely "places," but they deserve mention in this chapter because of their usefulness to the learner. A variety of organizations in your community provide opportunities for you to collect information or to gain new skills, groups like the Red Cross, scouts, Audubon Society, Sierra Club, YMCA and YWCA, and Big Brother. You can attend classes, lectures, and even participate in field trips. These groups also provide you with an opportunity to learn by doing, coming to master ideas and experiences by participating in them. Of course, you may have to join some organizations in order to participate in their activities. If you want to learn to identify birds, go with the members of the Audubon Society on one of their weekend field trips. If you want to learn to build a fire and get along in the wild, join the scouts and go on a weekend survival. There are also many opportunities for you to work as a volunteer in your community, in which case you will not only learn new skills but help other people as well. Your local chamber of commerce or United Way fund drive can provide you with a list of the many groups that operate in your area.

The Place to Be

I hope this chapter has persuaded you of the value of places in learning. There's a treasure chest of ideas, information, and experiences awaiting you in the schools, shops, museums, businesses, parks, organizations, and governmental agencies in your home town. It's *the* place to be for the young learner.

7 Learning from Research

Igor, the faithful assistant, scurries about the laboratory adjusting dials on monstrous machines, while the mad Dr. Frankenstein laughs hideously. At the doctor's command, Igor throws a giant switch, and on the operating table, the figure of a giant man twitches. Its eyes flicker open and it growls menacingly.

*   *   *

Benjamin Franklin is flying a kite in a thunderstorm. Lightning crackles all about, then *zots* its way down the kite string. "Eureka," cries Ben, "I have invented electricity!"

*   *   *

A twerpy little man in a white coat pours drops of brightly colored liquid from a test tube into a beaker. A puff of smoke rises. "At last," the twerp says, not even looking at his laboratory helper, whose spectacular beauty is almost hidden by her owlish glasses, "on the 12,467th try, we have discovered the antibacterium that will save New York from this mysterious plague."

What images do you see when someone says "research"? The portraits I have drawn are what we call *stereotypes,* fanciful but inaccurate views of the research worker. Because of the stereotyped portrayal of researchers on television and in the movies, many people carry about false images of them as madmen diabolically plotting to go against the laws of nature, or as geniuses whose seemingly crazy behavior benefits all of humankind, or as nerds who would rather fuss with laboratory apparatus than kiss a beautiful woman.

Research is not as glamorous as it is sometimes portrayed on television, and it is certainly much more diverse. Although there are people who spend their working hours in white coats in laboratories, there are all sorts of researchers in the world, including those who work with books rather than test tubes and people who spend time out on the streets living and talking with people rather than cooped up in a laboratory.

My practical definition of research is this: "What you do when you run out of answers." When you can't find the information you need, you turn to research to discover answers for yourself.

In earlier chapters I have explored some of the ways in which you can find answers to your questions by studying book and nonprint sources (Chapter 4), learning from people (Chapter 5), and studying at places (Chapter 6). But sometimes the answers give out. You reach a point where you can't discover what you want to know by reading in the library or by asking other people. There are times, too, when you simply don't have the resources available to answer questions, so you have to figure things out for yourself.

In fact, *you* are already a researcher.

As you are riding to school, your bicycle starts making a loud metallic noise. You stop, poke around, and discover that the chain guard is rubbing against the pedal crank. You find a stick and bend the guard back into position so it no longer scrapes.

*   *   *

While looking for an after-school snack you run across some lime sherbet, canned mandarin oranges, and chocolate syrup. "I wonder whether that would taste good?" you ask, and so you try out the combination and give some to a younger brother or sister to taste as well.

* * *

You've been reading in the newspaper about problems kids are having with drug addiction. You talk to some of your friends about what they think, then write a letter to the editor of the paper explaining what you believe should be done to prevent drug abuse among people your age.

Those are three examples of how you might conduct research as a part of your everyday life, research done without a laboratory or test tubes or elaborate equipment.

---

* * * QUESTING * * *

Think of yourself as a practical researcher. What problems have you faced *today* that you've solved on your own? It may have been as simple as discovering how to tie your shoes with a broken shoelace, or how to answer a problem in your history or math book, or how to get burned-on grease off a frying pan. Make a list of some of the problems you've solved today. What sort of research did each one involve?

Research and the "Scientific Method"

The American Association for the Advancement of Science observes that "Science is more than a body of facts, a collection of principles, and a set of machines for measurement; it is a structured and directed way of asking and answering questions (McGavack, p. 17). Although "research" and "science" are not identical, in this chapter I want to explore what is called the "scientific method" of looking at the world to figure out how things work. As Hy Ruchlis, an outstanding science teacher, has written, ". . . scientific method is the basic set of procedures that scientists use for obtaining new knowledge about the universe in which we live" (Ruchlis, p. 7). He might well have simply said "people" instead of "scientists" and "research method" instead of "scientific method," for as I have already shown, most people already use some "scientific" processes in solving or "researching" everyday problems.

In its simplest form, the scientific method consists of three broad stages:

> Posing a problem or question
> Experimenting
> Reaching conclusions

You *raise a question* about something you want to discover, *experiment* to see if you can find some possible answers, and *reach a conclusion* about whether your solution works. For example, in the case of the noisy bicycle, you *questioned,* "What's making that noise?"; you *experimented* by bending the guard back; and you *concluded* that your cure was a success when the noise stopped.

Actually, *experiment* is a too broad a term for the middle part of research. Most scientists and researchers agree that experiments also consist of stages or processes:

> Collecting data
> Forming a hypothesis
> Testing the hypothesis

A *hypothesis* is simply an educated guess about what's going on, based on the information you have at hand.

I have shown the scientific method in Figure 7-1, depicting it as a kind of research machine, where you put problems in one end and get solutions out of the other. You'll see that the experiment stage is drawn as a cycle to show that you may have to do a number of different experiments to come up with an answer that is satisfactory.

For instance, if your experiment of bending the bicycle chain guard

FIGURE 7-1: The Scientific Method

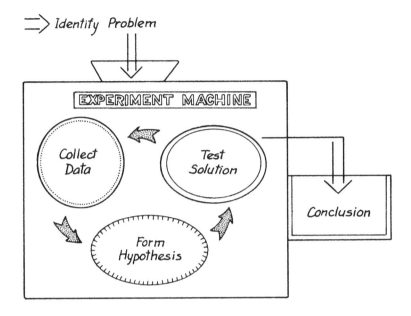

back didn't stop the noise, you'd look further, collecting more information, and maybe you'd find that you had a broken link in the chain or that the pedal was out of alignment. Then you'd form and test a new hypothesis.

It is important to recognize that researchers use the scientific method in many different ways. As David Killeffer has explained in his book, *How Did You Think of That?,* the Greek philosopher/ scientist, Aristotle, was the kind of thinker who would first create a hypothesis, then look for data that would show whether or not he was right. The British philosopher/scientist, Sir Francis Bacon, liked to collect lots of data and run numerous experiments before coming up with a proposed solution.

What matters most, though, is the attitude of the researcher/scientist that says, "If I look at a problem long enough, and if I collect information and check it out carefully, I can come up with a reasonable solution." In a way, that's a very bold kind of statement to make, for it places a great deal of faith in human ingenuity. In our century, however, the successes of science and technology give good evidence that the scientific approach to research does produce results.

Researching a Problem

To illustrate how you can use research in your own learning, I'll discuss some ways in which you solve three very different kinds of problems.

Problem I: Kitty Nibbles.
> While watching television, you are intrigued by a commercial that shows a bunch of cats racing to gobble down Kitty Nibbles Brand Cat Food while ignoring Brand X. You wonder if Kitty Nibbles is really that good.
> *The research question:* Do cats really prefer Kitty Nibbles?

Problem II: Television Violence.
> You've read an editorial in the local newspaper that says television is too violent for children to watch and that it is changing youngsters' values by making them prone to violence.
> *The research question:* Does TV really breed violence in young viewers?

Problem III: Sports Skills.
> You want to develop your skill in some sport. Perhaps you want to be able to shoot fouls more accurately in basketball or kick a soccer ball more accurately or dive with greater precision.
> *The research question:* How can I perform that skill better?

In Chapter 2, I discussed question asking in detail, so I won't review that here. I will note, however, that the great physicist, Albert Einstein, once observed that "the formulation of a problem is often more essential than its solution" (Killeffer, p. 43). Before you begin doing some research it's important to raise a number of questions and narrow them down into one you genuinely want to answer.

Problem I, Kitty Nibbles, is the sort that lends itself to a fairly common sort of "scientific" research. To find an answer, you'd need to set up a controlled experiment, probably using your cat as the "guinea pig." Although many people have objected to the use of live animals in experiments, in this case Tabby gets a pretty good deal, since the entire experiment will provide it with food.

One way to do the experiment would be to give your cat two identical bowls, one filled with Brand X, one with Kitty Nibbles. Which one does the cat choose regularly? Or you could observe carefully to see whether the cat empties out the Nibbles bowl before turning to Brand X. Or, I suppose, you could even listen to see if the cat purrs more loudly when given Nibbles than Brand X.

Right away, though, you can probably think of some problems in conducting this kind of research. For how many days would you need to run the experiment to be able to conclude that your cat prefers one brand or another? Would seven days prove anything? What could you conclude if the cat doesn't follow any pattern at all? What bearing would the tastes of your cat have on the Nibbles claim anyway—how do you know if your cat is typical of all catdom?

You can see, too, that record keeping would be very important in this experiment. You'd need to rule columns in a notebook to keep detailed records of what the cat was eating. Consistency would be important as well, so you'd need to feed the cat at about the same time every day, the same quantity each time, etc.

Eventually, though, you'd be able to form a reasonable conclusion based on your experimentation.

Problem II, TV Violence, is more difficult. In fact, I'll tell you right now that specialists in children's behavior have been trying to get answers to that question for years, and they are still conducting experiments. There is no clearcut answer, or at least answers that apply to *all* young people. Nevertheless, you could still do some research right in your own home to come up with some tentative answers for yourself.

It probably wouldn't be easy to set up a nice experiment like the Kitty Nibbles challenge. Instead, you might want to use some of your skills as an interviewer or poll taker (see Chapter 5) to talk with younger brothers and sisters. When you found them fighting, you might ask them why, or whether they think it's okay to fight because of TV. You might watch some TV along with them and observe their reactions: Do they get excited when a cartoon character is blown to bits? Do they cheer or laugh when people get shot or beaten up?

If you wanted to collect some statistics about violence on TV, you might make a count of the number of fist fights and shootings that take place on a typical evening of prime-time viewing. You might also maintain records on how much you and your brothers and sisters watch TV and which programs you prefer. Is there a pattern? Do people in your family prefer violent or nonviolent shows?

Eventually, you would collect enough information that you could create a hypothesis. You might not come up with an absolutely certain answer (and you would certainly want to test your hypothesis by continuing to observe what is going on), but you would be able to make informed statements about what's happening in the world of TV and young people's lives at your house.

Problem III, Sports Skills, suggests an interesting kind of research. Let's suppose you wanted to become a better diver and have a chance to make the school swim team. There are many places you could go for help. You might read up on diving, and you would certainly try to get some help with coaching. But you'd reach a point where practice would be needed for improvement, and practice is, believe it or not, a kind of experimentation.

You would dive ten times, fifty times, one hundred times, and each time you would collect a bit of information about what you were doing right or wrong. Along the way you'd try a series of experiments to improve your form and style:

"Maybe if I arch my back more on entry into the water I'll go in cleaner."

"Maybe if I don't bounce so high I won't flip over."

"Maybe I'm making my approach too fast."

You would be doing experiments every time you took a dive, learning each time. Eventually, you would start drawing conclusions—perhaps even subconsciously—from these trials, and your diving would improve. In general, if you approach a skill like diving with a "scientific" attitude toward learning, you'll learn faster than if you just dive a thousand times and hope for the best.

---

* * * QUESTING * * *

Now think about some of the questions and problems that you'd like to answer. Flip through the pages of your Learner's Notebook for topics that you think might lend themselves to research and experimentation right around home. Some could be very simple questions:

"What's the best time to take the dog for a walk?"

Others might be much more complicated:

"What's the best way to study for a test?"

They might involve other people:

"What's the best fast food?"

They might involve you alone:

"What can I do to clear up my complexion?"

First, list a number of questions about each problem that you'd like to solve; then list some possible experiments that you could conduct. Remember that some might involve "scientific" tests, like trying different acne medicine for a month at a time. Others might use experiments based on observing and interviewing, such as talking with your friends about their religious beliefs.

Finally, *do* the research. Collect information carefully. Write down your hypotheses and consider whether or not the data you are collecting will help you reach a sound conclusion. Don't be discouraged if some of your experiments don't prove much of anything; keep on designing new ideas and approaches and pretty soon you'll be able to come up with some answers that you can back up with your own research.

Drawing Sound Conclusions

And then there's the story of the guy who was sitting on a park bench, tearing newspapers into strips, throwing them into the air, and shouting, "Booga booga!"

"Why are you doing that?" asked a passerby.

"To scare away the elephants," came the answer.

"But there are no elephants in a city park!" said the passerby.

"See, it works!" said the guy.

Maybe not. The guy throwing newspapers in the air had fallen into a thinking error; the term for it (in Latin) is *post hoc:* reasoning after the fact. He assumed that since there were no elephants around, the newspaper scare was working. However, as you figured out already, it was not very likely that there were elephants in the park in the first place. He had reasoned backward and made a false conclusion.

A lightning bolt crashes down near your house and the lights go out. Is there a connection?

You wear your yellow socks to school and get an A on a mathematics test. Is there a connection?

You eat a tomato that tastes odd to you and you are sick the next day. Is there a connection?

It's sometimes very difficult to know whether one event actually causes another. In the case of a noisy bike, it might be pretty easy to identify the chain guard as the cause, but have you ever had one of those squeaks on a bike that you just can't track down, that seems to come from nowhere?

Sometimes research is a bit like trying to find that squeak.

There is also a problem that comes about because as a researcher, you sometimes want a particular result. You want to discover that Brand X tastes just as good to your kitty. Or you want to believe that all the murder on TV is having no influence on your younger brother or sister. Sometimes, then, our biases as researchers get in the way, causing us to overlook information that doesn't fit our particular system of beliefs, and when that happens, we get wrong results.

* * * QUESTING * * *

Research in Everyday Life

In his book, *Science in Everyday Life,* William Vergara offers scientific explanations for a number of common events or happenings. You could read the answers to the following questions in Vergara's book, but how would you go about conducting research to figure out answers on your own?

Why does bread get moldy?
How does antifreeze work?
Why does sound travel better with the wind?
Why does aspirin sometimes cause an upset stomach?
Why does moving air feel cool in warm weather?
How do nonstick pans work?
What are cosmetics made of?
How do meat tenderizers work?
What makes water boil?
Why are some dogs shy and unfriendly?
How do lightning rods work?
What are rocks?

See what you can discover as a researcher. Check out your answers by reading Vergara's book or an encyclopedia or a school textbook. Does your research match up with the work that has actually been done to answer these questions?

American humorist Artemus Ward identified still another research problem when he said, "It ain't so much the things we don't know that get us in trouble. It's the things we know that ain't so" (Huff, frontispiece). Most of us carry around ideas that, for one reason or another, are wrong. Sometimes these ideas were passed on to us as "words of wisdom" that we never questioned; sometimes they are just ideas that we've followed for so long that we have come to believe them. Think of the obstacles that Christopher Columbus had in trying to persuade people that the earth was round. Even though he had plenty of evidence before the voyage to prove his case, he had to sail off to the west in order to shake people's beliefs. It is important, then, for the scientist/researcher to go into his/her studies with an open mind, being ready to reject old untruths.

In his book *Is It Really So?*, Dwight Ingle summarizes some "tests" that a number of researchers apply to their experimentation to see whether conclusions are valid (pp. 81-88). First of all, a good piece of research must account for all the facts. If bending your chain guard stops the clatter, but only when you are going uphill, then you need to experiment to find a fuller explanation.

Good research must also be reproducible, which simply means that if you or another person do the experiment again, you'll get the same results. Before you announce to the world that Brand X tastes better than Kitty Nibbles, you might want to have somebody else do the same experiment with other cats to see if he or she gets the same kind of results.

A good experiment may allow you to make accurate predictions about what will occur next. On the basis of your cat food research, for example, you would predict that a neighbor's cat, borrowed for the occasion and given a choice of Brand X or Kitty Nibbles, would choose Brand X. Borrow a cat and try it! Does your research let you predict accurately?

Finally, good answers to questions sometimes (but not always) have a kind of simplicity to them. William of Occam, an English philosopher of the fourteenth century, came up with a principle that has become known as "Occam's razor." Given two explanations of the same thing, Occam hypothesized, the simpler one is probably correct. He advocated slicing away the more complicated explanation. To return to that creaky bicycle, for example, there are at least two possible explanations:

· Your chain guard is bent and needs to be fixed.
· Invisible creatures from Mars have taken control of your bicycle.

* * * QUESTING * * *

In *How Things Don't Work,* Victor Papanek and James Hennessey have been very critical of design engineers, who, they say, are more interested in making things look pretty than function well. Papanek and Hennessey point out that the average bathtub "doesn't work" in the sense that the faucets and handles are placed where they can stab you in the back or prevent you from stretching out to soak comfortably. They are also critical of kitchen cabinets, automobile construction, electric carving knives, and lawn mowers. You can extend your interest in research by looking around you and examining objects that are either broken or don't work as well as they might. The *problem,* then, is something that doesn't work. The *hypothesis* that you create is a guess as to how it could be made to work or work better. The *test,* obviously, is to do it! You might have a look at:

Toasters	Can openers
Refrigerators	Chairs
Electric clocks	Door locks
TV controls	Toys
Forks and knives	Chopsticks
Bookends	Typewriters

William of Occam's razor would suggest that the chain guard explanation is the better one because it is simpler. (The chain guard explanation is also better because it is based on observable data and you can reproduce the experiment. That doesn't prove there are no invisible creatures from Mars, but the truth doesn't seem to require them, at least in bicycle repair.)

If your research passes those tests, then you have reached the final stage of the research process, and you have a conclusion that you can use for your own purposes. In research, if a conclusion becomes widely accepted, pretty soon it becomes a principle or even a law, which means that people assume it is true without going back to do the research over again. Sir Isaac Newton's observations about objects in motion, made more than four hundred years ago, were accepted that way, thus allowing us to speak of the *law* of gravity.

Researchers are always tentative about their conclusions, which is to say that they are prepared to accept better answers. Henri Poincaré, a French philosopher/scientist observed that "a theory is good only as long as it is useful" (Killeffer, p. 143). We must always be ready to reject an old idea in favor of a new one. Thus in this century, Albert Einstein made discoveries in physics that led him to question Sir Isaac Newton's laws. Though we still talk about the "law" of gravity, we now know that Einstein's theory of relativity demonstrates that in some instances, that "law" is not accurate; relativity theory is the new "law," and presumably at some time in the future it, too, will be rejected in favor of a better explanation of how things work.

A Guide to the Young Researcher

With the completion of this discussion of research and experimentation, we come to the end of the how-to-get-information chapters of *The Young Learner's Handbook*. A summary of where we've been is given in Figure 7-2, a "flow chart" of approaches to learning. (A flow chart is something a scientist or engineer or business person uses to make certain he or she doesn't forget any important steps in a process.) This chart simply reminds you of all the places to search for information that I have mentioned in the various chapters. The chart ends with more learning to show that learning never really comes to a final, definitive, absolutely conclusive, once-and-for-all answer to questions.

FIGURE 7-2:   A Flow Chart for Learning

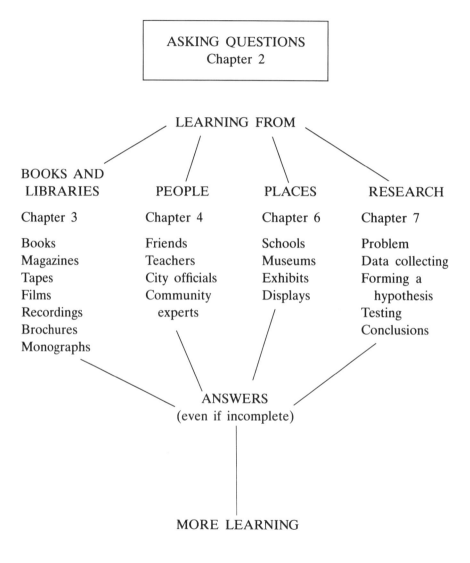

---

* * * QUESTING * * *

The advice people give is, in a sense, a conclusion that is arrived at through research. Sometimes advice is good, and it works well for others. Sometimes advice is overgeneralized, meaning that it just doesn't apply to all situations. Bad advice, then, reflects poor "research."

Here is some advice that newspaper columnist Wes Smith has offered to college graduates. Test each one of these conclusions against the traits of good research I have listed in this chapter. How were these conclusions derived? What sort of scientific research could you conduct to see if the conclusions are good ones or not?

"They aren't kidding when they say, 'Wash whites separately.'"

"Buy an alarm clock that works."

"Eat good meals. Greasy burgers take their toll."

"Buy good stuff. It lasts longer."

"There is no such thing as a self-cleaning oven."

"Be nice to the little people. You are still one of them."

"At some point in your life, your family will be all you have. Treat them right."

The Unknown

"The natural history of science is the study of the unknown. If you fear it, then you're not going to study it, and you're not going to make any progress."

Dr. Michael DeBakey, *New York Times,* September 7, 1976

In *The Mysterious World,* Francis Hitching remarks about the amazing progress science has made in the last century, almost to the point that people have come to take a view of science as magic. Computers have some of this aura of magic about them. In one television advertisement a young computer enthusiast tells his mother— wrongly—"A computer can solve any problem." Scientists, Hitching continues, can*not* solve *any* problem:

> In many scientific disciplines, the more that is discovered, the farther the horizon of knowledge seems to recede. In others, the underlying assumptions have become so shaky that they will soon be discarded and replaced. All contain mysterious and uncomfortable facts which cannot be explained by conventional reasoning . . . (Introduction).

His list of mysteries in this Atlas of the Unexplained includes the death of the dinosaurs, the sources of life, instinct, who really discovered America, undecoded writings of the ancients, unidentified flying objects, and the Bermuda Triangle. Of course, some of these mysteries will eventually be unraveled (since he compiled his book in 1978, researchers have made great progress in figuring out what killed off the dinosaurs). Still, the point remains that there are limits to human knowledge and limits to what can be discovered.

For you as a young learner, that ought to make life all the more exciting, for there is more, much more to learn. The late J. Allen Hynek, a major researcher in unidentified flying objects, once said, "There is a tendency in the 20th century to forget that there will be a 21st century science . . ." (Lewis, p. 238). Most young learners reading this book will be alive in the twenty-first century and doing the important work of their lives.

You are one of the important researchers, knowers, and learners of the twenty-first century.

8 Applying What You Learn

Scholars make a distinction between "pure" and "applied" research. *Applied* research explores new ideas to create a new product, solve a problem, or invent something that people will find useful in their day-to-day lives. *Pure* research is not impractical or useless; nor is it necessarily any "cleaner" or higher minded than applied research. But pure research is conducted primarily to find answers for their own sake, for the general enlargement of human wisdom.

Actually, many pure researchers point out that their work often has practical payoffs, and there have even been many "spinoff" or accidental discoveries during pure research—the artificial sweetener saccharin was discovered this way. Applied research sometimes seems more glamorous because it leads to useful ideas and objects that can change our lives right away.

The very fact that you are reading this book indicates that you are, in some respects, a pure learner or researcher. The reader of this book is likely to be a person who is interested in knowledge simply for the fun of it, who enjoys accumulating information on a wide variety of topics. However, I also suspect that like most young learners, you have a strong bent toward the practical and the applied—you probably like to know how things work in the real world and you're interested in finding solutions to problems. You'd like your learning to be useful, not simply ornamental.

This chapter is concerned with applying what you learn, how to discover ways to use your knowledge and understanding in everyday life. Sometimes that may mean applying learning skills successfully in school to raise your grades. At other times, it may involve figuring out how to do things differently so your life goes more smoothly. It might involve inventions like a burglar alarm made from strings and tin cans to protect your room. Or it might center on thinking about family relationships and improving the ways in which you and your brothers and sisters get along.

To explore ways of applying your knowledge, I want to tell you about something called a *heuristic* (pronounced to rhyme with sure-istic), which is, in plainer English, a *discovery plan,* or guide to learning and to applying knowledge. A heuristic reminds you of what to do first, second, third, and so on. It is not meant to limit your thinking in any way, and you are encouraged to break away from a heuristic whenever your own imagination takes hold or when the plan doesn't fit the particular project you're working on at the moment. In this chapter I will present a series of heuristics—some plans for using knowledge to reach decisions, solve problems, create new ideas, set goals, use your leisure, and predict the future.

Decision Making

You make decisions every day of your life. Some decisions are practically automatic—like getting up in the morning. Other choices are not especially important in the overall scheme of things—like whether to have Rice Krispies or cornflakes. But increasingly you will be making decisions that shouldn't be automatic or done without thought and will influence the rest of your life. What should I choose for a career? Where should I go for further education?

Some people make major decisions relying on instinct or intuition—deciding on the basis of whether something "feels right." Certainly there's much to be said for trusting your emotions in many decision-making situations.

At the same time, it's very important that your decisions be *informed,* based on as much knowledge and understanding of a situation as possible. The first heuristic or discovery plan, shown in Figure 8-1, can help guide you.

There are many different kinds of decisions that you can make using this heuristic. I'll illustrate it in operation with a concrete and familiar example. The decision is this: *What kind of dog shall I get?* (You'll realize that other decisions preceded this one: first, a decision to have a pet; second, a decision that the pet would be a dog rather than a cat or a bird.)

Step One involves identifying the decision: *What kind of dog shall I get?* That might seem very simple and obvious at first, but there's more to it than meets the eye. I think it is useful to describe the decision in detail, maybe even telling a story about it:

> I've wanted a dog for years and years, but we lived in an apartment and couldn't have one. Now we've moved to a new city and we'll be in a house with a yard and my folks say it's okay to get a dog.

It's good to list some of your reasons for wanting or needing to make the decision and to think about the outcomes or results—how will things change as a result?:

> Having a dog will change my life, because I'll have to feed it every day and walk it and bathe it and give it flea powder. But I'm ready! I want that dog!

Most decisions can be broken into parts or segments. There are a number of factors that you want to take into consideration concerning dogs: breed, size, color, friendliness, trainability, food requirements, and so on. There are also many alternatives in most decisions, and in this case, you have literally hundreds of choices

----

FIGURE 8-1:   Discovery Plan 1: Decision Making

1. What is the decision you have to make?
   a. Describe it in detail.
   b. What are your reasons for wanting or needing to make the decision?
   c. What will be the outcomes or results?
   d. What are the parts of the decision? Can you break it into pieces?
   e. What are the alternatives in your choice? Is there more than one alternative? Are there several ways you can go?

2. What knowledge, learning, or information do you need to acquire to make the decision? What can you learn from:
   a. books and media?
   b. people?
   c. places and institutions?
   d. research and experimentation?

3. List and weigh the *pros* and *cons* of each alternative possibility, the *fors* and *againsts:*

Possibility 1		*Possibility 2*		*Possibility 3*	
For	Against	For	Against	For	Against

   Give each *For* one to four stars * ** *** **** to rank its importance to you.
   Give each *Against* one to four minuses - -- --- ---- to emphasize its weaknesses and drawbacks.

4. Make your decision.

5. Determine how to evaluate the decision. How will you know whether your choice was correct?

----

among breeds. It is important not to cut off possibilities in decision making, so list all the options you can think of, even if some of them won't be realistic. (Okay, so you *know* a St. Bernard will be too big. But if you think you'd like one, list it; then you can look for similar kinds of dogs, but smaller.)

Step Two in this heuristic draws on your expertise as a learner. To make an informed decision, you need to do some studying. In your **Quest** to buy the perfect dog, you would probably go to the library and read about different kinds of dogs. You could also talk with people who own various breeds and get their opinions about a good choice. You might visit a dog kennel, the city pound, or a dog training school to learn more about various breeds and how they work out as pets. Could you conduct experiments to find out which dog to buy? Perhaps you could care for a friend's dog for a few days to discover whether that's the kind of animal you want around the house.

In Step Three, you argue with yourself. In the course of your learning you probably narrowed your choices down. Perhaps there are three or four different dogs you think would work well. At this point, it's helpful to pull together all your knowledge and list the *fors* and *againsts* for each dog on your list. What are all the good features? What are the drawbacks?

As you make this list you'll also realize that some factors are more important than others. A big dog eats a lot, but that may be compensated for by its affection or by the fact that you don't like little dogs. As you work with your list of fors, put stars ∗∗∗∗ near the items that you think are really most important. Give minuses − − − − to the againsts that seem most damaging. You might even want to recopy that list once or twice, putting the various considerations in the order of importance.

Step Four is the big one—decision time. Making the actual decision is never easy, and there's no magic heuristic that will make it for you. However, with the research and careful thinking you've done, you are in a good position to make a sound choice.

Step Five is evaluation, and that comes afterward. Did you make the right choice? Now, with a dog you've pretty much made an irreversible decision—you're stuck with what you got. But some decisions can be changed if they don't work out, and anyway, it's always a good idea to think about what you decided and why. If your choice of a dog is a good one (and there is every reason to think you will make the correct decision), you rejoice. If for some reason the dog

turned out to be a disappointment, you should ask, why? Was it because you didn't know enough about dogs in general? about this
breed in particular? Did you let its big brown eyes fool you into
thinking it would be a better pet? Did it just turn out to be a peculiar
dog—a "lemon"? In any case, by studying how you made decisions
in the past, you can learn to make better ones in the future.

✳ ✳ ✳ QUESTING ✳ ✳ ✳

What are the decisions you have to make or expect to make in
the coming years? List as many as you can. You might include
choice of:

Career   Job   School

Friends   Husband or Wife

How much money you want to make

Whether to cheat in school

Look at these decisions in terms of Discovery Plan 1. Think particularly about the Step Two, *learning*. What kind of learning do
you need to do to make these decisions as intelligently as possible?

Problem Solving

Figure 8-2 shows a discovery plan for *Problem Solving*. Like making
decisions, problem solving is very common; you do it day in and day
out. Some people panic when faced with a problem, or try to solve it
hit or miss. As a learner, you can put your understanding and knowledge to work for more rational problem solving.

In this discovery plan, you begin by describing the problem in detail, breaking it down into parts, thinking about the outcomes and
conclusions (Step One). Then you learn more about it following the
now familiar route through books and media, people, places, and
research (Step Two).

Step Three is crucial. Here you begin thinking of solutions to your problems. Just as no heuristic can make a decision for you, this discovery plan will not find solutions or make them for you. However, you can train yourself to exercise all your creative powers. Brainstorming is a good technique to use here (review Chapter 2 for a description of how it works). List as many solutions as you can, even ideas that seem far-fetched or unlikely. Get friends to add ideas to your list.

FIGURE 8-2: Discovery Plan 2: Problem Solving

1. What is the problem?
   a. Describe it in detail.
   b. Why is it important?
   c. What will be the outcomes of solving or not solving it?
   d. Break it into pieces—what are the various parts?

2. Learn more about it:
   a. from books and media
   b. from people
   c. at places and institutions
   d. from research and experimentation

3. Develop a list of possible solutions

4. Rate each solution, drawing on your learning. What are its:

Chances of Success

0   10   20   30   40   50   60   70   80   90   100%

List your solutions in order of their probable success. Which one will you try first? Which second?

5. Develop a "to do" list to put your solution into action. What do you need to do first? What next? Then what?

6. Put your solution into action and evaluate whether it works. If it doesn't work, try the next one on your list.

----

* * * QUESTING * * *

One common technique for exercising your creative skills is to list all the new uses you can make of a familiar object, limiting yourself to five or ten minutes. Get a sheet of paper and a pencil. Pick an object that you see around you or come into contact with every day and list ways in which you could employ it as a tool or helpful object. For example, what else could you do with a can opener? a pencil? a chair? a handkerchief? (*Bicycle U.S.A.* once published an essay on twenty-six things you can use a bandanna for while on a bike ride, ideas ranging from a flag when you need help to a bandage for a knee skinned in a crash.) Did you ever consider a handkerchief as part of a theatrical costume, serving variously as hat, scarf, necktie, or even mustache?

In Step Four of the problem-solving heuristic, you evaluate all the solutions. Put the most likely solutions at the top of your list. Take your time here, thinking (and drawing on your learning) to consider which seem to have the greatest chance for success.

In Step Five, you draw on your knowledge to work out a plan to put your solution into action. Here again, the heuristic can't help you come up with a "to do" list that will work. Brainstorming for ideas would be a good idea to create possibilities. It might also be useful to put the stages or steps on index cards that you can shuffle and reshuffle until you come up with an order that seems right.

Finally, in Step Six, you evaluate, and if your solution didn't work, you try another idea.

Let's suppose that your problem is study skills: You spend a lot of time working on history or geography or science but don't seem to get anywhere.

In Step One you describe the problem. Do you have a mental block about the subject? Are you too tired when you try to study? Is it noisy where you try to do your work? Is the subject matter too difficult or complicated? Is the textbook badly written? You list as many different parts of the problem as you can.

To learn more, you could check the library for books on study skills or possibly even find a self-help cassette on how to improve your learning or memory. You could interview teachers and friends, or you might go to a place like your school's learning center for ideas and pointers. Experimentation could be a part of your learning. You might get up early and try studying before school. You might look into renovating your home learning center so it's a place where you would like to spend more of your time.

From this study and experimentation you could eventually propose some solutions. Some ideas might be a bit on the wild or impractical side: "Quit school!" More sensibly, you might come up with eight or ten ideas that you think would have a good chance for success.

With this project, you could even put several of your solutions into action at once: changing your study hours, studying with a friend, not putting off study to the last moment.

Your grades, of course, would be a pretty good indicator of whether or not your plan was working.

Inventions and Applications

Ken Hakuta of Washington, D.C., sponsors an inventors' fair where creative people come to demonstrate their new products. At one show people came to display such odd and curious inventions as a cup that changes colors depending on the liquid that's put into it, a fly zapper that shoots insects out of the air with rubber bands, and a toy glider that returns to the flier like a boomerang. Hakuta himself made a fortune by marketing another invention, the Wacky Wall Walker: a plastic octopus that sticks to a wall when thrown and then walks down to the floor. Ken Hakuta says that inventors don't always get the support and publicity they need for new ideas, and he even sponsors a toll-free number where inventors can call to get a reaction to their ideas (Schneider).

* * * QUESTING * * *

What are the problems you'd like to solve? You might be having problems at school, with friends, with a hobby, with a sport you are trying to conquer. Try Discovery Plan 2 to see what strategies would be helpful.

Problem solving techniques can be used on topics that go beyond your immediate life or home town. Are you concerned about the problem of world peace? or the weapons race? or the supply of oil and gas? You can do some pure learning about these subjects, but you can also come up with possible solutions. By yourself you might not be able to do anything directly about something like the nuclear arms race, but as an informed citizen you could write your suggestions to a U.S. congressperson or senator and ask him or her for a reply.

The Ronco Company of New Jersey has been famous for selling interesting devices and gizmos on TV. Ronco developed the inside-the-egg scrambler, the pocket fishing pole, a portable high-speed mixer, a toothbrush that carries its own supply of paste, and a combination garbage can and chair that mashes trash while you sit (Covert).

Not all inventors deal with curiosities or novelties. At Michigan Technological University, for example, researchers have come up with ideas that sound a bit crazy but have direct applications in improving the state's economy. Biologists have discovered a bacteria, *Thiobacillus ferrooxidans*, that actually eats impurities in copper ore and makes refining less expensive than when it is done by machines. The scientists at Michigan Tech have discovered other bacteria that feed on wastes that are toxic to human beings, thus helping to solve the problem of waste disposal. Other researchers have learned how to make plastic from tree bark and have made "clones" of European trees that will grow faster and reach maturity sooner than they would ordinarily (Jackson).

Frank Piasecki is working on an idea called the Heli-Stat, which is a helicopter combined with a blimp. It flies rather slowly, but it has a tremendous ability to lift heavy loads, making it a useful tool in military service. Piasecki also has a $10.7 million contract to develop his invention (Sansevere). Unfortunately, as sometimes happens with inventions, this one did not work out in its trial runs, and in 1986 a prototype model of the Heli-Stat crashed, killing the test pilot.

One stereotype of the "inventor" is that of a person who is out of touch with reality, creating amazing but useless devices. Another stereotype is the one of the inspired genius who gets ideas when a light bulb goes on in the brain. Neither of these conceptions is particularly accurate. To create a new tool or object successfully, you need to know *how things work,* and that implies possessing knowledge. To develop something original, you have to know what has happened before, what has worked and what hasn't, and that, too, suggests mastery of information. If you want your invention to be anything more than a museum curiosity, you need to know what people want and need, what they will or will not find useful. (Ronco, by the way, was wrong in guessing that people would be willing to sit on their garbage. The company got stuck with 40,000 unsold trash mashers.)

The discovery plan in Figure 8-3 begins by having you assess what people need and want. Do people need a better mousetrap? a bicycle that doesn't fall over? In thinking of personally useful inventions and applications, you might think about what *you* need—a wastepaper basket that empties itself? something to write your school papers for you?

Once you've identified a need, your interest in learning takes over, and in Step Two, you do the background learning. A trip to the library would reveal that several books have been devoted to designs for better mousetraps, including little mouse hotels that are filled with (poisoned) food, so mice check in but not out. (You don't need to feel discouraged that other people have applied their intellect to this problem; the ultimate mousetrap is still to be invented.) A trip to the bike shop might teach you about adult tricycles that don't fall over, but you might also learn that these trikes are so heavy that

----

FIGURE 8-3:   Discovery Plan 3: Inventions and Applications

1. Learn about what people need and want.
    a. ideas
    b. objects and gizmos
    c. plans and strategies
        or
        Identify and learn* about problems that need to be solved.

2. Learn* about what has been tried but has proven only partly successful or a total failure.

3. Think about alternatives:
    a. Learn* about ways of doing things.
    b. Study ways in which ideas have been applied.
    c. Brainstorm for new ideas and solutions.
    d. Learn* how to put some of the brainstorms into action.

4. Select what seems to be your best solution.

5. Create plans and models.

6. Field test and evaluate.

7. Go public—make a fortune!

*Learn from books and media, people, places, research, and experimentation.

----

nobody wants to take them for long-range tours, thus leaving room for new inventions. As for the overflowing trash in your bedroom, you might respond to a TV ad and buy one of Ronco's 40,000 trash mashers, or you might decide that you can invent something better on your own. A visit to a computer store or your school's computer room might show you that although you can't get a computer to write your paper for you, several programs have been developed that guide you through the stages of the writing process and make writing easier, even down to checking your paper over for misspellings.

It pays, then, to research into past successes and failures in the world of inventions.

Step Three of the Discovery Plan is especially important: think about alternatives. Inventing is not just a matter of dreaming up terrific ideas; you have to base your inventions and applications on a sense of how to get things done. The scientists at Michigan Technological University didn't simply imagine a bacterium that would help refine copper; they had a background of research and knowledge and knew about many different curious kinds of bugs. If you want to build a better mousetrap, you'd better know a lot about mice and about traps.

In Step Four you pick what seems to be your best idea, and then you move on to a very important Step Five: creating plans and models and a prototype. This step may require a long period of time. Creating plans keeps you from going off in random directions (though you should feel free to alter your plans if they're not working out). It's a good idea to create a model, if possible, to work on some of the problems on a small scale before creating a prototype. Even if you are working with a new idea—rather than an invention—you can sometimes create models through games. Monopoly, for example, is a model of the world of finance, and there are many computer models or simulations of problems in the real world.

Finally, though, you'll have your invention or idea ready to go. In Step Six, you field test, which simply means trying it out under real conditions. Whenever you create something—whether an idea or an object—you will probably have to go through several trials to get it to work right. Field testing in real situations is especially important as a way of getting the "bugs" out of your work. In fact, as Victor Papanek has complained in his book, *Why Things Don't Work,* insufficient field testing is a major cause for consumer complaint. This failure helps to explain why brand-new products don't work quite right and why there are so many recalls of defective products; they've been sold before they were adequately checked out in the field.

Finally, after careful testing to make certain the product works, you can go public and make your fortune. Well, perhaps not a fortune. In fact, you may be doomed to be one of those inventors whose products only show up at fairs with those of other inventors. At the very least, though, you will have the satisfaction of having come up with a better way of keeping the trash under control in your study.

---

* * * QUESTING * * *

Be a dreamer! an inventor! a creator of ideas and schemes!

Look around for everyday nuisances and problems that could be relieved by a good invention; then create one. Think about life in school and invent things to help you do better there. Invent a better bookpack or briefcase; invent a scheme to get your homework done in school so you don't have to bring books home; invent a filing system for your notes that works better than the old way. Or look at any clubs or organizations you belong to and come up with some creative ideas to help them run better. Help your scout troop get better organized for campouts; invent a new lightweight tent that you can make at home; figure out a clever new way to attract members.

Remember that inventions can be bright ideas as well as gadgets.

Setting and Achieving Goals

What do you want to accomplish for yourself? Do you want to lose weight, build yourself up physically, become skilled at a sport, dance more comfortably, feel confident when you talk in class, know more about music, art, theater, politics? Use Discovery Plan 4 to establish goals and meet them.

The general process for a discovery plan is now familiar to you: identify the goals, break them down into parts, learn by every possible means, come up with a plan or a strategy, and then *do it*.

FIGURE 8-4: Discovery Plan 4: Setting and Achieving Goals

1. What is it that you really want to do? List some of the things you want to achieve.
   a. in your personal life—day to day
   b. around school—in class
   c. around school—outside class
   d. around your town or community
   e. in life

2. Choose a goal that you want to work on and describe it in detail. Break it down into as many parts and pieces as you can. Write down your reasons for wanting to achieve it. List some of the outcomes—how will your life change or become better as you reach this goal?

3. Learn* (need I say more?)

4. Develop a strategy or plan for achieving your aims. What do you need to do first, second, third? Create a timetable for accomplishing the various steps.

5. Do it and evaluate. Did you achieve your goal? If you fell short, what happened? Did your goal change as you learned more about it? Did you come to value it more or less as you made progress toward achieving it?

*Learn from books and media, people, places, research, and experimentation.

However, more has to be said about goals than just setting up plans and then learning how to meet them. With personal goals, particularly, it's just not as easy as it seems to achieve what you want. For instance, for about eight years I was a cigarette smoker, and for seven of those eight years I wanted to quit. My goal was clear, and I knew all I needed to know to quit: I had read the research on the harmful effects of tobacco, and I knew what a lifetime of cigarette smoking might do to me (making that lifetime a lot shorter, among other things). Yet I continued to puff away at a furious rate, until I got some outside help by going to a smoking withdrawal clinic.

There, the nurses and doctors helped me understand some of the reasons why I was smoking and gave me the help and support I needed to achieve my aim.

There are sometimes emotional blocks to achieving your goals, which is why, even though you might *want* to lose weight or to be more confident about talking in public you might have trouble doing it.

There are also some problems with setting *unrealistic* goals. Sure, you might like to dance better, but it would be unrealistic for you to set a goal of being as good as some of the dancers you see on TV. Certainly you'd like to be a first stringer on a sports team and maybe turn professional for a million bucks a year, but your body may just not be the type that will carry you that far. Sometimes people even set unrealistic goals as a way of protecting themselves against failure: if you aim impossibly high, who can blame you if you fall short?

Goal setting and achieving, then, involve a somewhat different sort of learning than I have discussed previously, a kind of knowledge and learning about yourself—who you are, what makes you tick, why you are the kind of person you are. I think you may find some of the following ideas helpful as you go about setting goals:

At first, let your imagination run free to create the best possible goals for yourself. It's okay to daydream about being the world's greatest ballerina or the finest baseball pitcher of all time as long as you don't start living in a fantasy world.

Then focus on *achievable* goals for yourself. You don't have to abandon the thought of being a good pitcher or ballerina, but do think about what your chances are. Don't focus on an impossible dream and then be disappointed that you can't make it. At the same time, don't underrate your abilities or be too modest. If you genuinely like to dance or have some natural ability at heaving a baseball accurately, think about becoming the best that you can be.

Analyze the *obstacles* in the way of achieving your goal. Some of the obstacles may be within you: maybe you are reluctant to practice as hard as you must to become good. There may be other obstacles: making a sports team is highly competitive.

List some ideas for overcoming those obstacles, one by one. Make a checklist for yourself. If mild laziness is your problem, think of ways to discipline yourself to work harder. If the school sports teams seem too competitive, think about some other places where you can gain experience.

Spend time thinking about your own emotions and the way they can tangle up achieving a goal. If you know your own feelings, you'll be in a better position to recognize some of the hidden problems that seem to crop up (like why I couldn't quit smoking when I knew it was bad for me).

Think of several alternative ways to achieve your goal. Here again your power as a creative thinker and learner comes in. There are numerous ways to quit smoking, lose weight, achieve excellence in a field. The more you know about the alternatives, the better your chances for success. Sometimes, too, you may have to adjust your goals. So you don't become the pitcher on the high school baseball team; you may still have a lot of fun as a pitcher in legion ball or in a softball league. If you don't make it as the prima ballerina in your school's version of the *Nutcracker,* explore other dancing opportunities in jazz or modern dance or dancing with friends for fun.

Planning Your Leisure Time

Experts predict that as we move toward the twenty-first century, people will have more and more free time. The length of the typical work week has decreased dramatically over the years, and as robots and machinery take over more and more jobs, there are prospects for even shorter weeks in the future. What will you do with the free time you have available?

What do you do with the free time you have available *now?* Do you lie around watching whatever's on TV, or do you use your time productively? Do you make every minute count, or do you find yourself saying, "I'd love to do that, but I just can't seem to find the time?"

For some people, there really isn't a great distinction between work and play, labor and leisure. Some love their work so much that it is constantly fun for them. (Some people find school a joy, for example, so home*work* is really not work at all.) Others treat their leisure time as if it were work—you've probably run into people who take their hobbies or sports much too seriously, losing all the joy in the process.

To use your leisure well, you may want to explore some of the possibilities using Discovery Plan 5.

FIGURE 8-5:   Discovery Plan 5: Exploring Leisure Time

1. Determine how much leisure time you have:
     a. Big chunks of time (most of a day)
     b. Middle-sized chunks (an hour or two)
     c. Bits and pieces (ten minutes to a half hour)
     d. Stolen moments (a minute or two)

2. Learn* about leisure time activities:
     a. In school vs. out of school
     b. At home vs. on the town
     c. Entertainment or activities provided by others
     d. Auto-entertainment
     e. Sports and hobbies
     f. Community resources
     g. Music, TV, film
     h. Books

3. Rank order your leisure time activities. Which bring you most pleasure or satisfaction?

4. Subdivide activities by the categories in 1 above: those which require sustained time, those which require less.

5. Organize to make maximum use of your free time.

*Learn from books and media, people, places, research, and experimentation.

A good starting point here is to find out just how much time you have for nonwork activities.

---

* * * QUESTING * * *

Keep a log in your Learner's Notebook for a week or more, just jotting down the times and amounts of free time you have. I suggest you think about categories ranging from chunks that are many hours long (probably on a weekend) to the odd moments that you might not even be aware of, like a few minutes between classes or the fifteen minutes before supper when nothing seems to be going on.

Look at it another way: if you sleep eight hours a day and go to school six hours a day and do homework four hours a day, there are still six hours per day not accounted for. Six hours is a surprisingly large amount of leisure time for you to explore. Your task in this **Quest** is to find out where that time goes.

Next, do some learning about leisure time activities, what's available in school through extracurriculars and outside school through clubs and organizations. You might list entertainment sources available in your town, but also consider *auto-entertainment* (which is *not* entertaining yourself in a car)—entertainment in which *you* are the center of things: playing a musical instrument, working on the martial arts, woodworking, painting, singing. List sports and hobbies that interest you; list goings-on around your town and community; list favorite television programs and consider how the movie theater can provide you with a productive kind of leisure time.

I want to put in a special plug for books (and other reading) as a source of leisure time activity. Reading is an especially good way to fill those small leisure moments, the few minutes that pop up in your day. If you develop the habit of carrying a paperback book around with you, you'll discover that just reading it in bits and pieces will allow you to cover a great many pages during a week. Magazines and newspapers also provide you with an excellent source for leisure entertainment, especially since you can frequently read through a short article in just a few minutes.

Once you've listed and learned about possibilities, rank order them in Step Three, and, in Step Four, break them down into time categories—those that need big chunks of time, those that could be done in a few spare moments.

Then, based on your learning, organize your leisure. Of course, you don't want to become so terribly organized that you don't ever seem to have time for just plain relaxing—there's much to be said for unplanned leisure time. But do make certain that you are using the free moments of your life to their fullest.

Predicting the Future

You don't really need a crystal ball to see the future. Although there will be surprises and unpredictable events, a good learner also has an edge on other people by being able to make accurate guesses about what may happen in coming years. Knowledge is the key, for the future flows from the present, and people who know the present can figure out the direction of that flow.

Discovery Plan 6 will help you organize your ideas as a futurologist.

In Step One, you choose a topic for exploration. To take an example close to home, you might want to make some predictions about what you will be doing for a living ten or twenty years from now. To take an example of international scope, you might want to try to predict the likelihood of a nuclear war taking place.

Step Two involves breaking a topic down into parts. What are the considerations in a job choice? Money would be one. Pleasure would certainly be another. Your present abilities and aptitudes would certainly figure into the prediction. Is it likely that you will get a job right out of high school or will you go on for further education? That, too, will affect the kind of job you have.

FIGURE 8-6:   Discovery Plan 6: Predicting the Future

1. Choose an area or topic that you believe will be of interest and importance in the future. This might have to do with your own future, the future of your friends and family, the future of your community or even the planet.

2. Think about and list the various parts or aspects of the topic; break it down into a list of subtopics.

3. Learn* about the topic, its past, its present, its projected future.

4. Write or think about some scenarios, short scripts or stories that sketch out what you believe might happen. Consider, what if:
   a. things change dramatically from now until then?
   b. things don't change?
   c. things change for the better?
   d. things change for the worse?
   e. the totally unexpected happens?

5. When you have written your scenarios, rank them in terms of your best guess about their probability, the likelihood that they will actually happen.

6. Read some science fiction about your topic—see whether other prophets agree with your projections.

7. Wait around a few months or years to see whether your predictions come to pass.

*Learn from books and media, people, places, research, and experimentation.

The question of nuclear war can also be broken down into parts. The development of weapons systems will be important. You may know, too, that defense against weapons systems may play a role (if you don't know that, Step Three will take care of it for you). The strength of various countries will probably be a factor, and you might have one category that just has to do with whether or not people truly want and are willing to work for world peace.

Step Three involves learning from every source you can think of: learning about careers, learning about nuclear weapons systems.

Step Four is something new: it involves writing (or thinking through) *scenarios*. Think of a scenario as a miniature short story, one where, based on your knowledge of the present, you think about how things will go in the future. The discovery plan lists some of the variations that you might consider: whether and how things change and whether they change for the better or the worse. A scenario does not have to be very long and it doesn't have to be a literary work of art, but it should contain all the essential details of your prediction.

In an enjoyable variation of scenario writing, you might even want to write a science fiction or futuristic story, complete with plot and characters. Imagine a short story written about yourself and your work when you are thirty-five or forty years old. Consider a story about what might happen with nuclear war if international relationships improve (or write about the alternative if things get worse). Make your story the best possible prediction (or scenario) of what you think the future will hold. You might also enjoy reading science fiction or essays in which other writers guess at the future. Ask your librarian to help you locate works on your topic.

It is difficult to evaluate a prediction, because you have to wait around to see whether or not it comes true. Nevertheless, predicting is a valuable way to exercise your mind and your knowledge. It is one of the ultimate tests of your skill as a young learner.

* * * QUESTING * * *

This chapter has taken us beyond thinking about learning to considering how learning can be applied in the real world. I've really only touched the surface with such topics as problem solving, decision making, inventing, the use of leisure, predicting the future, achieving goals. The **Quest** that is most important now is for you to begin moving off on your own to think about applications. Sometimes school seems pretty removed from your day-to-day concerns, and what shows up on television may seem a lot more engaging than reading one more chapter in the social studies book. Without appearing to try to make a sales pitch for school (education has to sell itself to learners, I believe), it would be useful for you to think about applying your learning in school to issues, problems, and concerns in the real world, combining that with your own interest in learning independently. This **Quest** is not something that you can write down in your Learner's Notebook. Rather, it is an attitude or state of mind that keeps you mentally alert, always probing, asking why, looking for deeper answers, thinking about how things connect and what makes them important or valuable.

It is a **Questing** frame of mind.

9 Sharing What You Know

A French philosopher and economist, Anne-Robert-Jacques Turgot wrote in the 1700s about how learning is shared: ". . . speech and writing . . . have made a common treasure-store of all individual knowledge, which one generation bequeaths to the next, a heritage constantly augmented by the discoveries of each age" (*Progress of the Human Mind,* in Adler and Van Doren, p. 976). Language, he said, permits people to share ideas and information, so we can avoid having to "go back and reinvent the wheel" every time we want to learn something new. From your **Questing** you know about the rich supply of information that is available to you encapsulated in print and media forms—books, magazines, TV, films, tapes. You also know of the incredible amount of information that is passed along by word of mouth, information you can obtain from people through interviews, polls, and casual discussion.

I hope, too, that you have come to see yourself as a knowledge *maker,* a person who can find or create answers to your own questions. In the passage just cited, Turgot made no mention of an obligation to share your ideas and experiences with other people, but many of us feel that such an obligation exists. I like to think of people here on earth as a community of learners: each of us has special interests and skills and knowledge, and as we gather ideas and information, we have a duty to share that learning with others.

Sometimes the sharing is *required,* as in school, where you may be assigned reports or must present your knowledge in a paper or report. You can use your skills as a young learner to good advantage in school, and I will offer some suggestions to improve your performance in school as part of this chapter. However, I am more interested in *voluntary* sharing of information, where people contribute to the storehouse of knowledge because they want to and because they know other members of the community of learning want to learn of their discoveries.

Sometimes the exchange of information can be informal, for instance, when you tap a friend or family member on the shoulder and start talking because you just *have* to share something exciting that you've just thought about or read. At other times the sharing is more formal, as when you write or prepare a talk or display from which interested people can learn.

Human beings are powerfully curious critters. You'll find that if you are interested in sharing your learning, there is a range of people ready to listen. It's largely a matter of seeking them out and beginning to contribute to Turgot's "treasure-store" of knowledge.

Displays and Exhibits

Much learning is based on collecting things. This may be a collection of notes based on reading and interviews; it may be a collection of tape recordings of people talking; it may be a collection of objects or artifacts that contribute to your understanding. One way of sharing knowledge is simply to display a collection of materials, with some guidelines to help other people understand their significance.

Hobby collections—butterflies, model railroad cars, stamps, bubble-gum cards—are a good place to begin thinking about ways to prepare an exhibit. Other people can learn a great deal from your hobby, but not if it is a jumble. Arranging a collection is not just a matter of being neat or coming to discover artifacts that you'd forgotten you owned. It is a way of organizing knowledge.

If you collect stamps, for example, there are a number of different ways to put them on display. If your stamp collection consists of a shoe box filled with a thousand stamps, a good first step is to spread the stamps out on a large table (away from curious cats and children or breezy open windows) and to sort them into patterns and piles. What stamps seem to go together? Can you see some similarities and differences that allow you to separate the stamps into different categories?

Some stamp collectors like to divide their holdings by national origin, which gives you interesting insights into the postal systems of various countries and the kinds of pictures nations choose to put on their stamps. Other collectors prefer to go by chronological order, which helps them understand how postage stamps have evolved, how they have changed over the years. Some collectors are interested in *themed* collections, looking at, say, boat stamps from all over the world or animal stamps or stamps featuring political leaders. Remember, the way the collection is displayed is a way of structuring the knowledge within. (See also Chapter 3, "Data Gathering," for discussion of ways of learning from artifacts or objects.)

The techniques of how to prepare a good display are too detailed to be included here. You can find books in the library that will guide you, and you can frequently learn about good display techniques at a hobby store, where you can buy materials or guidebooks that will get you started or improve your own collection. You can also learn from other collectors by carefully studying their displays.

A P.S. on collecting: even if you get tired of your hobby, don't throw the collection away. Put it safely in a box or trunk to share with your own kids some day. I guarantee they'll be interested in seeing what you did when you were young, and thus you can share your learning with them. Further, collections have a tendency to

---

* * * QUESTING * * *

Think about sharing information by organizing and displaying any collections you've developed over the years. (You've probably been saying that you want to get the stuff organized sooner or later anyway, and here's the opportunity.) Look at the materials and think about the best way to display them—in your room or elsewhere—so other people can get the benefit of learning from your collection.

Or, if you're one of those well-organized people who has kept up with the collection, spend some time looking over what you have done. What does the way that you've organized your collectibles say about what learning you've done and about how you see the world? What can you do to improve the structure? Perhaps it is time for you to do some tidying up and some labeling so others can get all the meaning and understanding that is hidden away in your collection.

---

grow more valuable with age. The stamps or railroad cars that you collect today may become quite valuable collector's items twenty-five years from now.

Other Displays and Exhibits

Not all displays come from hobbyist collections. As you've engaged in learning **Quests,** you've probably accumulated ideas and information on a wide range of topics: community activities, state and national politics, science or mathematics or art or music. You may find a number of opportunities to exhibit your work.

Many communities put on annual *science fairs* where young learners can exhibit the results of their scientific research and experimentation. There are a number of good books available describing ways of creating excellent science fair projects (for example, see Thomas

*** * * * QUESTING * * * ***

Many collectors band together to share ideas and information and to display their collections. You can find clubs for collectors of stamps, license plates, bicycles, magazines, photographs, and even old-fashioned flat irons. If you have been a collector/hobbyist, consider joining the community of learners who share that interest. The local library may have information on such clubs, or you can simply ask around school and town until you locate the name and address of the club or an officer. Joining a hobby club is a good way to encourage yourself to improve your collection while learning an extraordinary amount from other people.

Also, collectors' clubs often have regional or state meetings where you can go either to display your collection or to be dazzled by the collections other people have prepared. Clubs will sometimes sponsor exhibits in community centers and libraries.

Moorman's book, *How to Make Your Science Project Scientific,* listed in the bibliography). Frequently ribbons and cash prizes are awarded, and if you're interested in furthering your education in science, there are even college scholarships available to some winners. More important than prizes, however, is the opportunity to share your research, to see how your interests fit in with those of other people your age, and to learn from and teach other people in this community of learning.

In my city, an annual *youth talent fair* displays the work, not only of young scientists, but of young architects, draftsmen, artists, writers, dancers, musicians, woodworkers, and craftspeople. Most regions or states have similar art and crafts displays.

Sometimes there will be a young people's display at an art fair being held in your community, or there will be special displays in bank lobbies, school board offices, or other community gathering places. Museums frequently display the work of young people and even sponsor fairs or contests for projects based on local or regional history or culture.

4-H clubs are interested in young talent and sponsor displays of scientific agricultural research as well as arts, crafts, and homemaking skills. Scouting and youth clubs often have exhibits and carnivals to display the products of learning.

Speeches, Talks, and Demonstrations

Speech is one of the oldest and most effective ways of sharing information. In some parts of the world, people still rely primarily on *oral* language—word-of-mouth—to share ideas, information, stories, even literature. Although our culture uses print to store information of permanent value, oral language—talking face-to-face or on the phone—is the form most often used to transmit ideas and learning. As video and laser disk technology become more and more sophisticated, we can guess that we may drift more and more to a high-tech oral culture.

Gossip and chitchat are one way to share ideas, and most of us spend a lot of time in this sort of talk. "Chatter" can be idle and aimless, but it also serves important purposes. We often use it informally to talk through ideas that are forming in our heads and to see whether or not we've gotten those ideas on track. Even scholars and researchers use conversation to share their thoughts with colleagues, and many will say that some of their best ideas come in the coffee lounge rather than in the laboratory or library.

Speeches and demonstrations are a way of sharing information that falls midway between casual conversation and writing things down on paper. In a speech or talk you plan out what you want to say in advance. Some people like to write out a speech and read it to the audience, but it is generally more effective to make some notes and use them as a guide as you talk to an audience. Because people are there in front of you, you have a chance to adapt what you are saying. If the audience looks puzzled, you can go over your ideas using different words. You can answer questions right on the spot, too, as a way of insuring that people understood what you were saying.

School gives you plenty of opportunities to learn speaking skills and provides some chances to practice, so I won't go into the techniques of public speaking here. However, it's important to note that a lot of people—young and old—find speaking in public quite difficult. It's scary to stand up in front of a group of people while all eyes are focused on you. Generally, confidence in giving talks develops with practice, but the ideas about learning presented in this book can also be helpful to you as you prepare talks and speeches.

It's an important confidence builder to realize that you really *know what you are talking about,* that your learning is substantial. Some kids prepare for school speeches by looking up a few ideas in the encyclopedia or reading an article or two in a magazine or newspaper. While it may be possible to get away with such minimal preparation, I would hate to do it myself. No wonder underprepared speakers get nervous or don't sound very articulate behind the lectern.

On the other hand, if you've really plunged into a topic, learning from books, people, places, and especially from your own research, you're bound to be more confident. You may even have the happy experience of your talk seeming to "write itself"; that is, you know the subject so thoroughly that the form of your presentation comes to you naturally. And if you are knowledgeable, you'll certainly be in an excellent position to respond to questions from your listeners when you've finished your speech; you won't be embarrassed by not knowing answers. There's just no substitute for good learning when you prepare to go public with your talk.

Your learning **Quests** will often provide you with materials to supplement your presentation through demonstrations or audio-visual aids. The underprepared speaker doesn't have much to go on other than the materials he or she found in the encyclopedia. The learner who has truly **Quested** into a topic may come to a speech with various kinds of artifacts—posters, advertisements, or objects that demonstrate a point. You may supplement your speech with tape recordings of people you've interviewed, or you may have a colorful graph or overhead transparency showing the results of a poll or survey you've conducted. You may even be able to demonstrate an idea or scientific principle as you proceed.

Perhaps public speaking just isn't a skill that you want to develop or something with which you will feel comfortable. You might consider a tape recorded alternative. You've probably seen learning tapes for sale in bookstores or supermarket checkout lanes. These are speeches done in the privacy of a recording studio. Some museums have learning tapes that can be checked out to provide a kind of self-guided tour of the museum and its exhibits. You'll also see projects at science fairs and hobby shows that feature an expert's talk on tape to be played while people view the exhibit.

If you have some good things to say, but the idea of public speaking makes you uncomfortable, you might think about doing a learning tape.

Photo Displays and Slide Tapes

"One picture," goes an ancient cliché, "is worth a thousand words." Like most clichés, this one is both accurate and inaccurate. It would not be correct to argue that a photograph conveys *exactly* the same message as spoken or written language. It is safe to say that often a person can study a picture and learn an enormous amount from it, perhaps even more than could be learned by listening to an informed person.

In any case, photography provides excellent opportunities for you to share what you know. Consider the camera, then, as a tool that you can use to share information. You can photograph your scientific experiments while they are under way; you can take pictures of the people you interview as part of a poll; you can snap pictures of objects that you'd like to "collect" but which are too heavy to carry home; you can photographically record your own collections that are too bulky to move.

It's possible you'll want to prepare "stand alone" photographic displays—just putting up pictures for people to study. However, you will often find it handy to mix media, using photographs with other forms of communication. Most photography displays in art museums are carefully labeled or captioned. (A picture may be worth a thousand words, but a good label is what makes a picture comprehensible to other people.) You can use photos along with your speeches and talks, and certainly your writing will be much more effective if you can use a photograph or two for illustration.

An especially effective mixed media presentation is the slide tape, which coordinates colored slide photographs with a prerecorded cassette tape. Many schools and clubs have projectors that can be programmed with a signal on tape to change slides at exactly the right moment. There are also controls for multiple projectors that allow you to flash two or more slides at once or in rapid succession or to do dissolves and fades from one slide to another. The cassette tape itself can include your talk about the slides and what they mean, but it can also have recorded music, interviews, background sounds, and so on. Learning tapes that you make yourself can also be combined with slides to create an exciting presentation.

To learn more about the possibilities of photography as a way of sharing information, check your library or talk to the salespeople at a good camera store. You may also want to learn about any camera clubs that are organized in your town or school. Photography may turn out to be not only a good way for you to share your learning, but a hobby you'll want to pursue in its own right.

Although I've emphasized *photography* in this section, "pictures" include drawings and paintings. If you have an artistic flair, use that talent just as you would photography. You can illustrate ideas and concepts, include sketches of people and places, present portraits.

Films and Videotapes

If one picture is worth a thousand words, how many are sixteen pictures a second worth? That's the speed at which movie projectors show pictures to create the illusion of motion. A television screen flashes multiple images per second, thousands per hour, millions in a week of television viewing.

Home film and video technology has put the use of these media within your grasp. Although you may not own the equipment, you can probably borrow it from school or church or club. Many communities with cable television even have public access studios where you can make visual presentations at little or no cost.

In just the past few years, portable television cameras and recorders have become so widely available that few people think very much about making home movies. However, if you have access to an 8-millimeter film camera, you can do some interesting things. You can, for example, keep the camera steady and take a picture every few seconds or minutes or days to speed up the motion of a process like a flower opening or a seed germinating. You can create your own animated cartoons by clicking off pictures of your drawings a frame at a time, each frame showing a bit of motion. You can shoot fast sequences in slow motion to reveal the fine details of a process. Ask at your library or photo store to find some good books and pamphlets on how to create quality movies using 8-millimeter equipment.

Video equipment will allow you to do many of the same things. In addition, most video cameras allow you to record sound along with images, giving a fuller re-creation of the experience. With video you can speed things up and slow them down, freeze frames, and zoom in and out for super closeups and wide angle shots. Some video cameras will let you print titles right on the screen, and others include editing equipment that will let you remove or reorganize parts of a tape for a high quality final product. You can add background music to some videos, and many of the techniques useful in slide tapes can be incorporated comfortably in a video production.

It's very important, however, to learn how to use movie and video cameras *well*. With still photos, it's easy enough to toss out bad pictures and select only those that are truly worth a thousand words or more. Because the film or video camera is running constantly, it's much more difficult to get high quality material. Have you ever seen a bad home film or video, with bouncing camera, shots of the ceiling, and pictures of people looking self-conscious or waving goofily at the camera? You want to try to avoid such amateurism in your video or movie work.

Again it's beyond the scope of this book to go into much detail about TV or film production; there is plenty of advice in print and many people available to advise you. Try to keep your attention and camera focused on the idea that these visual media are ways of sharing what your know. The quality of your film and video will be enormously improved if you don't simply shoot scenes for their own sake. Know precisely what you are interested in conveying to an audience and then aim to get the pictures you need to enhance your demonstration.

✳ ✳ ✳ QUESTING ✳ ✳ ✳

Explore using technology for presenting your knowledge. Think about some of the **Quests** you've been doing. How could you use a cassette recorder to share information? (See also Chapter 3, "Data Gathering.") Can you make use of a movie camera or video recorder? Can you shoot some colored slides or make some color prints? Can you make drawings and sketches of what you see as important? Then work on ways to incorporate your data in an impressive public presentation.

✳ ✳ ✳ COMPUTERQUEST ✳ ✳ ✳

Computer programs are now being written to help people display and present information. Some computers now will let you do animation sequences on screen; most have "art packages" available that let you put professional graphics on the screen to illustrate your points. There are optical scanners that let you digitize pictures and transfer them to the computer screen (or printout), and some computer programs will let you or let a viewer/user proceed through a presentation at their own rate or select the kind of information they want to receive. (The first computer I owned was purchased based on a "buyer's helper" program designed for me by a seventh grade student.) If you're a computerphile, explore ways of using the computer to present ideas and information.

Writing

Despite computers, video cameras, laser storage disks, and telephones, one of the most common ways of presenting information in school and in the real world remains the *report.* School reports come in many different kinds. If you haven't already been assigned one, the odds are that you will soon have opportunities to write research reports.

As a young learner, a **Quester,** you should now find report writing something right down your alley, a fast ball right over the heart of the plate. You know about research techniques; you know about ways of applying knowledge in the world; you know about the importance of sharing information with an audience. While many of your schoolmates will head off to the encyclopedia section of the school library and do an ordinary job of copying down the facts, you can use all your skills as a learner to write reports that are genuinely interesting and lively, that show you have not only studied the basic facts of a subject, but have made sense of them and have done learning on your own.

Sometimes when young learners start to write reports, odd and curious things happen to their language: it loses its freshness and starts getting stuffy, sounding more like an encyclopedia than a person.

One cure for that is to make certain you choose research topics that genuinely interest you. (Most teachers will give you a choice of topics, so spend time thinking about ways to make the report on a topic that you're excited about.) It is also useful for you to think of report writing as a kind of *storytelling* about your learning: you can tell your readers how you came to learn what you know, how you interviewed people and conducted experiments, how you discovered interesting books and materials.

One of the skills you'll need to master as you write reports is *documentation,* which simply means listing where you got your ideas and information. In school reports, especially, you'll learn about making references (statements that explain where information came from) and bibliographies (a list of books at the end of your report). In this book, I've put the references to various books in parentheses, for example, (Smith, p. 36); these refer back to items in the bibliography. (Flip to the final pages of the book to see how a bibliography is arranged.)

There are many different forms for documentation, and usually the teacher will give you specific instructions on the form he or she wants you to use. In general, your rule of thumb should be to include enough information to permit another person to locate the resources easily.

More important is for you to develop the habit of good record keeping as you do a research project. You can use your Learner's Notebook or your school notebook to keep lists of the books you consult, the people with whom you speak, the places that you visit as part of your quest. Don't take shortcuts at this stage or rely on memory.

There are many ways of putting ideas in writing besides the report. Think about writing as a way of sharing ideas that can be every bit as interesting, exciting, and dynamic as a video production. For example, if you are interested in the world concern for nuclear arms control or the control of nuclear power facilities, consider that you could just as easily write a play as a report about your findings. Instead of a term paper, you might create a short story or a piece of science fiction about your ideas. Poetry is a good way to convey emotions and ideas in a powerful and compact form. You can consider writing scripts for radio drama that you present on tape recorder.

Some interesting ways of presenting ideas through writing are shown in Figure 9-1.

You can also write for publication to find a broader audience for your ideas. Many editors of school newspapers are eager to receive letters and guest editorials. So are some local newspapers, and if you are a letter writer, you can quickly find yourself in print. You may write for newsletters published by hobby interests or clubs, and you might even write an article on some aspect of your hobby that could be published in a national magazine.

If you're interested in exploring all the possibilities open to you, let me encourage you to look at a companion book, *The Young Writer's Handbook,* which my wife and I wrote together (Tchudi and Tchudi). You can also get good help from such magazines as *The Writer* and *Writer's Digest,* and you can find helpful books at the library that will provide you with information on how to write particular forms— books for children, for example, or science fiction—and how to find a place to publish your work. In the spirit of this book, too, you can look for people in your community who know how to write and like to write. There are a great many writer's clubs, where people who like to write get together to share their ideas, and you can certainly make contact with people who have managed to become published and who would like to share their learning with you.

FIGURE 9-1:   Some Forms of Writing

Reports
Profiles or sketches
Reminiscences (memory papers)
Autobiography (your life story, or parts of it)
Monologue (one person talking)
Dialogue (two people)
Conversations (several people)
Scripts (plays, TV programs, radio shows)
Parody (making fun of something by imitating it)
Poetry (haiku, cinquain, rhymed, unrhymed)
Essays
Editorials
Advertisements
Riddles
Posters
Telegrams
Letters
Critical reviews
Newspaper or magazine articles
Interviews
Campaign speeches
Petitions (a request for somebody to take action)
Stories (fiction or true-to-life; science fiction, historical fiction,
adventure, fantasy)

✳ ✳ ✳ COMPUTERQUEST ✳ ✳ ✳

The great new tool of the writer is the computer word processor, which allows you to type on the screen and make as many changes as you want before printing a final copy. There are programs available as well that help you check your spelling and offer suggestions about the style of your writing. Unquestionably, computers are making the physical part of the writing process a lot easier for people. You can also use a computer word processor (or a specially designed program) to store and file your notes and drafts. You can save your writing on a computer disk and then have someone else—teacher or friend—look at it and add suggestions. You can put your writing on display by way of telephone modem so that a network of people can read it and add comments or suggestions and questions. A growing area of interest in computers is "desktop publishing," which allows you to lay out a professional looking page—including graphics as well as text—on the screen before printing. Thus you can use your computer not only to write but to print copies of a hobby newsletter for yourself and a few friends. Explore all the possibilities of the electronic wizard that sits there winking its cursor at you.

Appendix:
Forming a QUESTARS Club

In many respects learning is a solitary activity. What goes into your brain and remains there is an individual matter, entirely up to you.

However, that doesn't mean that learning has to be lonely or done only by individuals. Some of the most successful research projects have been conducted by teams working on the simple principle that two (or many) heads are better than one.

If there are other people your age around school or town who seem to share some of your own interests, you might consider forming an organization of learners. In my area we've created several after-school study groups which we've called **Questars,** after **Questing** and "reaching for the stars." You are cordially invited to form a chapter of Questars International.

What a **Questars** chapter does should be largely up to the members. So will the rules and regulations you want to create for yourselves. I suggest that at your first meeting you determine two things:

What kinds of officers do you need? Does your club need a president? (Maybe you could call him or her a **Questmaster** or **Questmistress** instead of president?) You'll probably need some sort of secretary or **Questnoter,** and, if your club collects any materials, you may want to appoint a librarian or **Questarian.** Will you need a treasurer (or **Buckquester**)?

What will you investigate? Here it might be useful to review Chapter 2, "The Art of Questioning," and do some ballooning or brainstorming to see what interests the members of your club have in common. Of course, you could each go your own way and share the results of your **Questing,** but doing research and exploration with every member of your club taking responsibility for one part or segment makes the learning go a lot faster.

When you've settled on a topic, decide what steps you are going to take next. Get some of your members to take responsibility for looking into print and media resources. Other people may be responsible for visiting places (though you may also want to do this as a group). Still others might line up some people to be interviewed (or, perhaps, to be invited to your club meetings as a guest).

Can you find a regular place to meet? Perhaps somebody's parents will let you have a corner of a basement or attic as a place to store your club's records and perhaps to display your projects when they are completed. Or you may want to organize as an after-school club, in which case you might be able to get part of a classroom to store things. (Working through school gives you an advantage, too, in that you may be able to use some of the school's equipment, whether a video camera or a science laboratory.)

Consider the possibilities of group entries in science fairs. Your club may develop a local reputation for good work, and that, in turn, will be good in helping you get new members.

Speaking of members, you may want to make a membership card for each person in your club. One possible design is shown in Figure A-1.

FIGURE A-1: **Membership Card Design**

Bibliography

Adams, James L. *Conceptual Blockbusting*. New York: W.W. Norton, 1979.

Adler, Mortimer and Charles Van Doren. *Great Treasury of Western Thought*. New York: R.R. Bowker, 1977.

Ahl, David, ed. *The Best of Creative Computing*. Morristown, N.J.: Creative Computing Press, 1978.

Blake, Jim and Barbara Ernst. *The Great Perpetual Learning Machine*. Boston: Little Brown, 1976.

Bransford, John D. and Barry S. Stein. *The Ideal Problem Solver*. New York: W.H. Freeman, 1984.

Covert, Colin. "Amazing Ronco Scrambling for a Future." Detroit *Free Press*, January 27, 1984, 1B, 3B.

DeBono, Edward. *Lateral Thinking: Creativity Step by Step*. New York: Harper Colophon, 1973.

Friedenberg, Edgar. *The Vanishing Adolescent*. New York: Dell Publishing Company, 1959.

Fuller, Buckminster. *An Operating Manual for Spaceship Earth*. Carbondale, Illinois: Southern Illinois University Press, 1969.

Harrison, Allen F. and Robert M. Bramson. *Styles of Thinking*. Garden City, N.Y.: Doubleday, 1982.

Hitching, Francis. *The Mysterious World*. New York: Holt, Rinehart, and Winston, 1976.

179

Huff, Darrell. *How to Lie with Statistics.* New York: W.W. Norton, 1954.

Hutchens, Robert Maynard. *The Learning Society.* New York: Praeger, 1968.

Ingle, Dwight J. *Is It Really So?* Philadelphia: Westminster, 1976.

Jackson, Luther. "Michigan Tech Adds Ideas to UP Economy." Detroit *Free Press,* January 20, 1986, 1, 8.

Jorgensen, James D. and Timothy F. Fautsko. *QUID: Quantified Intrapersonal Decision-Making.* New York: Walker and Company, 1978.

Katz, William. *Your Library.* New York: Holt, Rinehart, 1979.

Killeffer, David H. *How Did You Think of That?* Garden City, NY: Doubleday, 1969.

Koberg, Don and Jim Bagnall. *The Universal Traveler.* Los Altos, California: William Kaufmann, Inc., 1974.

Lehman, Karl. *Thomas Jefferson: American Humanist.* Charlottesville, Virginia: University of Virginia Press, 1965, 1985.

Lewis, Alec. *The Quotable Quotations Book.* New York: Thomas Y. Crowell, 1980.

McGavack, John, Jr. and Donald P. LaSalle. *Guppies, Bubbles, and Vibrating Objects.* New York: John Day, 1972.

McLuhan, Marshall. *Understanding Media: The Extensions of Man.* New York: McGraw-Hill, 1964.

Michigan State University Libraries. *Term Paper Research Guide.* Library Instruction Series No. 14.

Moorman, Thomas. *How to Make Your Science Project Scientific.* New York: Atheneum, 1974.

O'Brien, Robert and Joanne Soderman, eds. *The Basic Guide to Research Sources.* New York: Signet Mentor, 1975.

Organization Development Software. *Consultant.* Des Plaines, Illinois: ODS, Inc., 1985.

Papanek, Victor and James Hennessey. *How Things Don't Work.* New York: Pantheon, 1977.

Paradis, Adrian A. *The Research Handbook.* New York: Funk and Wagnalls, 1966.

Polanyi, Michael. *Personal Knowledge.* Chicago: University of Chicago Press, 1962.

Polya, G. *How to Solve It.* Princeton, N.J.: Princeton University Press, 1945.

Postman, Neil and Charles Weingartner. *Teaching as a Subversive Activity.* New York: Delacorte Press, 1969.

Rivers, William L. *Finding Facts.* Englewood Cliffs, New Jersey: Prentice-Hall, 1975.

Rothrock, John. *How to Research Any Subject for Any Purpose.* White River, Vermont: Rothrock Associates, 1976.

Ruchlis, Hy. *Discovering Scientific Method.* New York: Harper & Row, 1963.

Russell, Helen Ross. *Ten Minute Field Trips.* Chicago: J. G. Ferguson, 1973.

Sansevere, Bob. "Blimp-Copter Is a Monster." Detroit *Free Press,* January 27, 1984, 4A.

Schneider, Karen. "Fathers of Invention," Detroit *Free Press,* January 19, 1986, 1A, 10A.

Schroeder, Fred. *Designing Exhibits: Seven Ways to Look at an Artifact.* Nashville, Tennessee: American Association for State and Local History, 1976.

Smith, Wes. "Attention, Graduates! Here's Some Sage Advice As You Leave the School of Soft Knocks for the Real (Shudder) World." Chicago Tribune Press Service. Detroit *Free Press,* June 9, 1986, E1, E3.

Tchudi, Susan and Stephen Tchudi. *The Young Writer's Handbook.* New York: Charles Scribner's Sons, 1984.

Vergara, William C. *Science in Everyday Life.* New York: Harper & Row, 1980.

Wheeler, Michal. *Lies, Damn Lies, and Statistics.* New York: Dell Publishing, 1976.

Whitehead, Alfred North. *The Aims of Education.* New York: Signet/Mentor, 1963.

Windley, Charles. *Teaching and Learning With Magic.* Washington, D.C.: Acropolis Books, 1976.

Witherspoon, Bruce. *The Second Mammoth Book of Trivia.* New York: A & W Visual Library, 1982.

Index

Adult education, 108
Applications, 28
Applied research, 135–157
Aristotle, 122
Art, 72
Artifacts, 37–38
Audio recorders, 47–51
Audio-visual equipment, 71
Aural learning, 8

Bacon, Sir Francis, 122
Ballooning, 22–25
Bermuda triangle, 134
Bibliography, 179–181
Biography, 79
Book learning, 8
Books for young adults, 79
Bookstores, 75–76
Brainstorming, 26–27
Bramson, Robert, 21
Bulletin boards, computer, 100
Business schools, 108

Cameras, 51–53
Camp, summer, 108
Card catalog, 64–67
Catalogs, 72
Charitable organizations, 116–117
Civic organizations, 116–117
Clerk, city, 109
Collections, 37–39, 160–162
Colleges and universities, 106–109
Columbus, Christopher, 128–129
Commerce, 113–116
Communicating, 158–173
Community education, 108
Community, learning, 101
Community notebooks, 72
Comparisons, 28
ComputerQuest, xiv, 25, 58, 76, 100,
    169, 173
Computers: as research tools, 53–58,
    67–68; bulletin boards, 100
Conclusions, drawing, 127–131
Consumer information, 72

Conversation, 85
Curiosity, 1

Data file programs, 55
Data gathering, 35–58
Daybook, 43–44
DeBakey, Dr. Michael, 133
DeBono, Edward, 27
Decision making, 136–140
Demonstrations, 85–87, 163–165
Desktop management, 55
Dewey, Melvil, 65
Diaries, 43–46
Discovery learning, 8
Discovery plans, 136, 138, 141, 146, 149, 152, 153
Displays, 159–163
Documentation, 45–46, 170
Drawing, 47

Einstein, Albert, 123, 131
Encyclopedias, 62–64
Exhibits, 111–113, 159–163

Fiction, 79
Filing, 41–42
Films, 71, 167–168
Filmstrips, 72
Friedenberg, Edgar, 105
Fuller, Buckminster, 2
Futuristic thinking, 28

Galeries, 111–113
Goal setting, 148–151
Government, 109–111
Graphics programs, 56

Hakuta, Ken, 143
Harrison, Allen, 21
Heli-Stat, 145
Heuristics, 136, 138, 141, 146, 149, 152, 153
High tech libraries, 67–71
Hitching, Francis, 133–134

Holograms, 70
Hutchens, Robert Maynard, xiii
Huxley, Thomas, xiii
Hynek, J. Allen, 134
Hypothesis, 121

Imaginative thinking, 28
Index cards, 45
Ingle, Dwight, 129
Interviews, 51, 87–90
Intuitive learning, 8
Inventions, 143–148

Journals, 43–46

Katz, William, 58
Killefer, David, 122, 123, 131

Lateral thinking, 27
Learner's Notebook, xv
Learning center, 4
Learning pattern, 9
Lectures, 85
Leisure planning, 151–154
Letters, 100
Libraries, 59–75
Library of Congress, 66
Local history, 72

Magazines, 77–78
Medical reference materials, 72
Metaphors, 28
Michigan State University, 102–104
Michigan Technological University, 144
Modems, 70, 100
Moorman, Thomas, 162
Morrill, Justin, 102, 103–104
Multimedia libraries, 70
Museums, 111–113

Newspapers, 77
News, television, 98
Newton, Sir Isaac, 131

Nonfiction, 79
Notetaking, 36, 43–46

Observation, 83–84
Observation schedules, 44
Occam, William of, 129–130
Opposite thinking, 28

Papanek, Victor, 147
Paper records, 40–47
Parallel thinking, 27
People, learning from, 80–101
Performances, 99
Phonemes, xi
Photo displays, 165–166
Piasecki, Frank, 145
Places, learning from, 102–117
Polls, 90–97
Post hoc reasoning, 127
Postman, Neil, 20
Predicting the future, 154–156
Principle learning, 8
Print resources, 59–80
Problem solving, 140–143
Pure research, 135

Questars club, xvii, 106, 107, 175–177
Questing, xiv; pattern for, 1–15
Questing activities, xiv, 6, 9, 14, 19, 21,
    27, 29, 32, 33, 39, 41, 46, 48, 50, 69,
    71, 73, 75, 80, 84, 85, 86, 91, 93, 96,
    97, 107, 109, 114, 116, 120, 126, 128,
    130, 133, 140, 142, 144, 148, 153, 157,
    161, 162, 168
Questioning, 17–34
Questions, interview, 89
Questions, unanswered, 31–33; framing
    for library search, 61–62

Reading, xi–xii
Reading notes, 45
Recordings, 71
Reference books, 72–75
Reference services, 71

Research, 118–134
Rivers, William, 58–59
Ronco Company, 144, 145
Roosevelt, Eleanor, 1
Rosten, Leo, 2
Ruchlis, Hy, 120–121

Samuelson, Paul, 17
Scavenging, 5–6
Schools, 104–106
Scientific method, 120–123
Sketching, 47
Slide tapes, 165–166
Speeches, 163–165
Stereotypes, researchers, 119
Superquestions, 30
Surveys, 90–97

Tactile learning, 8
Talks, 163–165
Telecommunications, 57
Telephone, 99, 101
Telephone directories, 72, 109, 114
Television, learning from, 97–98
Thinking: parallel, 27; metaphorical, 28;
    imaginative, 28
Topics for investigation, 12, 15, 16, 22,
    33–34, 68, 88
Training colleges, 108
Trivia, 18
Trivial Pursuit, 19
Turgo, Anne-Robert, Jacques, 158

UFOs, 134
Unanswered questions, 31

Venn diagrams, 23
Video bookstores, 76
Video cameras, 52–53
Videocassettes, 71, 98, 167–168
Visual learning, 8, 9

Ward, Artemus, 127–128
Weingartner, Charles, 20

Whitehead, Alfred North, 3
Witherspoon, Bruce, 18
Wooden, John, xiv

Word processing, 56–57, 173
Writing, 169–172